6 mindsets to lead
a high-performing
service team

SERVICE MINDSET

JAQUIE
SCAMMELL

First published in 2018 by Major Street Publishing Pty Ltd with the title *Creating a Customer Service Mindset*. This edition published in 2020.
PO Box 106, Highett, Vic. 3190 E: info@majorstreet.com.au
W: majorstreet.com.au M: +61 421 707 983

jaquiescammell.com

Quantity sales. Special discounts are available on quantity purchases by corporations, associations and others. For details, contact Lesley Williams using the contact details above.

Individual sales. Major Street publications are available through most bookstores. They can also be ordered directly from Major Street's online bookstore at www.majorstreet.com.au/shop.

Orders for university textbook/course adoption use. For orders of this nature, please contact Lesley Williams using the contact details above.

The moral rights of the author have been asserted.

A catalogue record for this book is available from the National Library of Australia

ISBN: 978-0-6486626-2-4

Internal design by Production Works
Cover design by Yianni Kouros
Cover photo by Prue Aja Photography
Printed in Australia by Ovato, an Accredited ISO AS/NZS 14001:2004 Environmental Management System Printer

10 9 8 7 6 5 4 3 2 1

Disclaimer: The material in this publication is in the nature of general comment only, and neither purports nor intends to be advice. Readers should not act on the basis of any matter in this publication without considering (and if appropriate taking) professional advice with due regard to their own particular circumstances. The author and publisher expressly disclaim all and any liability to any person, whether a purchaser of this publication or not, in respect of anything and the consequences of anything done or omitted to be done by any such person in reliance, whether whole or partial, upon the whole or any part of the contents of this publication.

Preface

The right service mindset is the foundation of sustainable success in service. This book was driven by my curiosity and desire to find Australia's unsung heroes: organisations who lead by example in the service space. From the Melbourne Cricket Ground to Bendigo Bank, I discovered that these businesses display six service mindsets which have fuelled their achievements. And, if you adopt these six mindsets, service can be simple.

When this book was first published in 2018 under the title *Creating a Customer Service Mindset*, it touched a nerve for many business leaders and appeared frequently on Australian business-book bestseller lists.

The book gave CEOs and general managers a strong starting point for shifting the mindsets of their workforce; they found it useful to imagine what service needed to look like in order for their businesses to excel in the 21st century.

- Human resource and business department leaders found that the various case studies, provided from multiple industries, offered practical insights into how other organisations were slowly shifting the dial in service.

- Individual frontline leaders told me that the reflection questions and activities were highly effective in getting their teams quickly aligned to a service mindset.

The book has been used in various contexts: business-to-business relationships, small business, large organisations, and by entrepreneurs seeking inspiration for themselves. The common thread in the feedback I've received has been that *Creating a Customer Service Mindset* provides invaluable information about building sustainable and dynamic businesses founded on great customer service.

The response has been so overwhelming, in fact, that I was prompted to expand the conversation and share more of my learnings in a three-book series. *Creating a Customer Service Mindset*, under its new name *Service Mindset*, becomes the first book in this series.

The second book in the series, published in early 2020, is *Service Habits*. Mindset and habits work hand-in-hand to embed behaviours that strengthen the relationships with those you serve. *Service Habits* tunes into the behaviours of service, exploring 27 habits for employees at all levels to learn and practice, offering an abundance of activities and techniques. Get your mindset and habits right, and you'll develop a *Service Culture* – the subject and title of the third book in the series.

Service Mindset, however, is where great service kicks off. This book will help you expand your consciousness and learn how to lead service in your teams, to achieve better results.

In service to you,

Jaqs X
jaquiescammell.com

Contents

*The less we see employees and customers as separate,
the more our service will inspire.*

*The less we see ourselves as separate from others,
the more we will want to serve.*

Foreword

Having a customer service mindset is essential for any organisation committed to improving and creating a sustainable operation. This book provides practical and profound insights into the processes and procedures that can help transform your organisation.

Customer service is the foundation on which great organisations are created. Customer service unites all employees to a common purpose focused around serving the customer. It propels the organisation to be driven by the market and provides the incentive to seek continual improvement and reinvention. But it is difficult. Few organisations have the discipline and commitment to embark on this journey and to use the voice of the customer as the driver of change. This is a journey that never ends – as you are continually driven to change and improve as customers' needs change. It requires you to become a truly learning organisation.

It starts with creating a customer service culture. A culture that is defined by values and behaviours that put the customer at the centre of how you act and make decisions. It requires you to define the behaviours that are required to delight the customer and create customer advocates for your organisation. This must include policies, procedures and processes that enable every employee to make the right decision for the customer.

Creating a customer service mindset requires a disciplined approach that must be implemented right across the organisation, and this book provides excellent examples of how a few Australian companies have approached this challenge.

Cultural change is essential – but you must also use the voice of the customer to drive product design, process improvement, quality improvement – all elements of your organisation. This is hard work, but it is essential to make your customer service transformation sustainable.

Service Mindset is unique in that it provides useful implementation suggestions that will allow any organisation to make quick progress.

Building trust in your organisation is difficult, but one of the important elements of establishing trust is customer service. Customer service forces you to confront the truth of how customers perceive you if you are willing to listen and hopefully take action.

I recommend this book as an important contribution to any leader wanting to build an exciting and dynamic organisation founded on great customer service.

David Thodey
Chair CSIRO and Jobs NSW and former CEO of Telstra and IBM ANZ

About the author

Jaquie Scammell is passionate about people and relationships. This is the heart of everything she teaches, and it's everything that superior customer service relies on.

She has spent most of her career living at the intersection of employee and customer, observing how the two relate; whether working on the shopfront floor of McDonald's when she was 16, to now as a sought-after speaker, facilitator and coach working with some of the largest global workforces in retail, banking and hospitality, as well as major airports, stadiums and events – from Wembley Stadium in the UK to the Australian Open Grand Slam in Melbourne.

Jaquie has managed and advised small workforces and large – the latter including those with over 9,500 staff, interacting with millions of fans on a daily basis. But no matter the size of the business, or how many customers they converse with, her observations and her message remain the same: you must create more meaningful relationships to increase your customer connection.

As you are about to read in this book, Jaquie's approach to transform your customer service culture, to decrease complaints and increase compliments, is much simpler and more human than better processes and procedures.

The mistake many organisations make is approaching customer service like it's an automated process, like we're robots in a factory machine. While, sure, organisations must have steps of service and systems in place, the real way you increase loyalty is through your frontline service leaders, the people who impact your customer service staff, who impact your customers every day.

When she's not researching these types of relationships, Jaquie practises mindfulness, yoga and other things that help her be a good human in any way she serves in life.

jaquiescammell.com

Acknowledgements

Given that gratitude is one of my character strengths, I could write a whole book on acknowledgements. However, I have narrowed this list down to the handful of people who truly inspired me, supported me and persevered with me during the creation of this book.

Matt Church and Peter Cook who created the incredible community, *Thought Leaders Business School* are first on my list. Thank you for giving me access to the tools and support network to make this book a reality.

The team at Qualtrics kick started the research for this book. They trusted me enough to open their client base up and introduce me to some brilliant organisations in Australia to interview. From this opportunity I met my Unsung Heroes who gave me their precious time and trusted me to come into their inner circle and explore what they do in their customer service space: Jason Bradshaw from Volkswagen Group Australia; James Heath and Andrew Cass from Australian Unity; Ian Jackman, Julie Dillon, Haylee Doering from Bendigo Bank; Cathy Jones from Healthscope; Adam Summerville from Emirates Leisure Retail Australia; and Rob Lorimer from CSIRO (although not an unsung hero in this book their interview was a valuable contribution to this book).

Kelly Irving was the voice of reality throughout the book writing journey. She guided me through with tough love, encouraged me to dig deeper, to set and meet my writing deadlines and get me to write my best work. Thanks to my publisher, Lesley Williams at Major Street, who placed trust in me to deliver a product she would be proud to sell.

Niki Flood has been an incredible support throughout the whole journey. She has been the perfect planner, diary manager, comforter and doer, which has allowed me to focus on the things that are important.

I also benefited from several conversations with Zara and Troy from Humour Australia, Oscar Trimboli and Dermot Crowley.

My Greek Angel, Costa Kouros, has supported me on this journey and on the greater journey of life. He has given me the space, pep talks and words of wisdom at times when I was jaded, exhausted and grumpy. Above all, he has had more belief in me than I have had in myself at times. He is one of the most service-minded human beings I have ever had the pleasure of knowing.

Finally, my father, who has shown me much in life, and yet the most profound impact he has had on me is showing me what it means to really serve. I will share his story and the impact it has had on many lives in my next book.

PART I
HOW TO SERVE

I n this age of digital transformation and technology, many argue we are more connected than ever before. In business, especially, artificial intelligence (AI), automation and the rise of robots has improved speed, efficiencies and processes beyond our wildest imaginations.

But at what cost?

Employees now provide products and services to consumers without ever having a face-to-face conversation. Customers type questions or issues into live chat feeds on websites, Facebook Messenger and other online conduits. We see more and more people in stores with headphones on, sending a strict message to service staff that they are not to be disturbed.

Our desire for speed and convenience is compromising our customers' greatest and basic needs as humans: care, kindness and one-on-one attention.

Service is simple.

Yet we have made it overly complicated. We have created complex systems and internal processes that, while designed to help our teams, often stop us from delivering the service we know our customers crave.

Like many other leaders and companies, you have probably tried – and failed – many times to operationalise your customer service culture. The reason? You have forgotten that human beings are unpredictable creatures and customer service is anything but routine and automatic.

Customer service is a privilege and those employees who interact with your customers on a day-to-day basis have the power to positively impact someone's life, not to mention your brand. Yet a lot of the time, especially in Australia, those interactions are negative.

Mediocre customer service is at an all-time high in Australia. Over one-third of customers surveyed in CPM Australia and the ACRS Omnibus Tracker's *The State of Customer Service in Australia Report* (see the resources at the back of this book for details) stopped shopping at a company in the year spanning July 2016 to June 2017 due to a poor customer service experience, and this number looks set to increase.

What can we do about this?

As you'll soon see, it is possible to have fast and meaningful customer service — and the solution is more innate than you may think.

When it comes to winning the hearts and minds of your customers, it's the behaviours of your frontline employees that influence your whole organisation's performance and results.

How customers *feel* when they interact with your employees and frontline staff determines how they *feel* about your company itself. This is what determines whether they will be a one-click wonder or a customer for life.

Procedures and steps of service may be great for robots and androids, but it's the ways in which your service staff act and the emotional connection they create with your customers that will determine your ultimate success.

These behaviours, this service mindset, starts with you.

LEADERS DRIVE THE TRANSFORMATION

Rather than look at complex customer service strategies and ways to engage your staff, this book talks to the heart of the most powerful and influential people in your business – you, the frontline leadership team.

As a leader, you are responsible for your people who are responsible for your results. Even if everyone in your organisation is already excellent at what they do, sharpening their emotional competencies and their behaviours at work will contribute to a service mindset that will give you and your organisation an extra edge.

When we are highly tuned in to the people in front of us we start to frame questions differently, pause before we speak and even start to see things from someone else's perspective. This conscious service environment transforms everything it encompasses and connects with: from head office to the shop-front floor, from one human being to another.

Leaders who operate with a service mindset help build a service culture: a high-performing culture where customer loyalty is constantly increasing. For many businesses, customer loyalty is seen as equal to risk management, financial performance and safety. In fact, if we were to replace the word 'customer' with 'humans', we could say that our goal in business is to create greater loyalty with other humans.

I have worked with tens of thousands of staff who serve hundreds of customers in environments such as Wembley Stadium (UK) and McDonald's, and at major events like the Australian Open and Sydney Olympics. If I were to sum up the golden rule of customer service I would say:

Be a good human every time you serve.

The thing leaders often forget is to show their team what that looks like. You need to get out of your heads, stop reading the rulebooks and remember the one thing you are here to do: to serve.

Many of my clients in banking and retail have realised the power of developing and nurturing this kind of service mindset. They have invested in defining and showing employees what best practice looks like when they serve in business. I have been very fortunate to be privy to what that looks like, and I will share that with you in this book.

Contained within these pages you'll find not only how to create a service mindset in yourself and your frontline staff, but you'll also read case studies and examples of real Australian organisations that are leading a superior customer service culture. They are the true unsung heroes of our industry, backed by research and data collected internally and externally over a period of time.

I am extremely proud to share these stories, to inspire many more small and large Australian businesses. Let's not leave it up to the global rock stars like Google, Amazon and Facebook. Let's shine a light on our own backyard.

The past is not a predictor of the future. To operationalise superior service in a world of robots and automation requires a methodology that is more human, more driven by our awareness of emotions and feelings than ever before.

We must be leaders of people, not results.

So let's look at how a service mindset can not only positively impact your organisation's service culture, but can change our lives and the world for the better.

IT STARTS WITH BUILDING RELATIONSHIPS

Customer service revolves around relationships. Developing the relationship between leaders and employees, as well as the relationship between employees and customers, is paramount to your success if you are to create a customer service mindset in your organisation.

In this first part of the book, we will look at why you need to be more connected to customer service in your organisations today, especially against a rising tide of AI and automation.

We'll look at how customer service in Australia measures up to the rest of the world and identify where many organisations are going wrong, so you can get it right.

The first step on the journey to creating a service culture is to assess what consistent and consistently good customer service actually looks like. So I'll introduce you to the skills and behaviours that make up the foundations of a superior service mindset, as well as exploring how these will help you gain a *cumulative advantage*, instead of a competitive one.

Ready?

1

Service is human

The sole meaning of life is to serve humanity.
LEO TOLSTOY

When I was fourteen years old, I was hungry to get out in the world and work. I craved independence, the thought of earning money excited me and I wanted to learn new skills. A locally run delicatessen was willing to employ me for a couple of shifts a week after school hours.

I will never forget my first week. I learned the different products such as deli meats and cheeses, and used the meat slicer. I had no problem serving customers with a smile and being friendly; however, there was one skill that I was not prepared for – receiving cash and giving change. It involved calculating the difference manually, with no calculator, no mobile phone and no digital POS (can you imagine?).

Fast-forward to the present, where mental arithmetic skills are no longer needed to work in a shop (and will likely never be again). Many manual customer service skills have been lost to technology. Yet good old-fashioned friendliness and care was needed then and it's still needed now.

So what role can a human play, now that purchasing a product can be achieved more cheaply, more accurately and faster? If we are unable to show care and be friendly in our service interactions, do we even have a role to play in service?

How does this impact the role of humans in service interactions in the future?

THE RETAIL REVOLUTION

The retail revolution has undoubtedly changed our lives. Some of the changes could, however, in some senses be considered losses. For instance:

- We no longer have to speak to people when going to the checkout in a supermarket.
- We no longer have to go into a shop and be helped by an assistant when buying clothes.
- We no longer have to walk into a bank and speak with someone to get a home loan.
- We no longer have rapport with the family-owned takeaway store, as we now see a different Uber Eats delivery driver every Friday night.
- We no longer have well-groomed, happy faces greeting us at the check-in counter when checking in for a flight.

Sadly, it is more than likely that a robot will replace the sales assistant role completely ten years from now, or perhaps even earlier, thanks to the acceleration of AI.

Today, all over the world, tasks are being automated to make transactions faster, more efficient and more consistent. Bit by bit, they are replacing traditional interpersonal service experiences. There are fewer strangers interacting with each other, fewer smiles being exchanged, fewer conversations adding depth and interest to someone's day, fewer relationships being formed.

Increasing rates and costs of materials for bricks and mortar stores, rent and, of course, labour rates all add to this dilemma. In the retail industry, in particular, traditional service models are being replaced by a mix of online and face-to-face inter- actions that attract customers who are looking for quick, convenient solutions.

In retail, in Australia, the 50-year-average growth rate revenue was 3.80%. The Australian Retailers Association reported that as of December 2017, that growth rate had dropped to 2.76%. Retail is doing it tough.

So at what cost are we willing to increase speed, efficiencies and consistency, to lose connections and relationship capital with our customers?

PROGRESS OR PROCESS?

The Future of Jobs report by the World Economic Forum pre- dicted that robotic automation will result in the net loss of more than five million jobs across 15 developed nations by 2020. It is said that the technological progress that we are cur- rently witnessing in this 'machine age' will see a jobless future for many humans who hold roles in retail and food services businesses.

Of course, this is a big topic and while at this point we are aware that roles in the service sector will be replaced by robots in the future, we are still unsure what *new* roles will be created during this transformation. Many of us feel like this retail robot revolution is still too far away to plan for.

Silicon Valley entrepreneur Martin Ford in *Rise of the Robots* states:

> The threat to overall employment is that as creative destruction unfolds the destruction will fall primarily on labour-intensive businesses in traditional areas like retail and goods preparation, while the creation will generate new businesses and industries that simply don't hire many people.

Personally, I see the benefits in automating many roles that are routine and repetitive. Routine means a set of tasks that can be codified in a program for computers and robots to perform. This enables considerable cost savings compared to the cost of human labour. It also means we can offer a consistent 100% guaranteed service or product. There is minimal wastage and increased productivity.

However, how do we humans *feel* when we purchase goods and services provided by a robot? For each new step forward with digital innovation and automation it feels like one step further away from human-to-human connection.

It's like we're driving through a tunnel in the most magnificent mountain ranges, for the purpose of getting to the desired destination quicker. By cutting out the windy roads we are gaining speed yet missing out on the scenery, the grandeur of what the mountains bring. We no longer experience that place and its surroundings with an associated emotion or a meaningful memory, it's just a long dark tunnel with measured lights and road markings.

We take the tunnel for a shortcut to speed and convenience, yet we miss out on the beauty and the interactions on the way.

A DIGITAL DOUBLE-EDGED SWORD

Budo (modern Japanese martial arts) has been described as a double-edged sword. It promises greater strength for the user if they can understand and embrace its duality: kindness versus strictness. That's how I see digital innovation – it is making our customer service stronger in many ways, yet it also comes with many risks.

In the rapid paced life of the Western world, customers value speed, efficiency and consistency, all of which have been proven to support customers to develop trust, and which ultimately drive customer loyalty. A great place to find speed, efficiency and consistency is anywhere there is a self-service option (just look at your local supermarket).

The question is:

Are we happier customers from these self-service digital interactions?

Over the last decade, the way we as customers interact with self-service technologies has been studied and we are now starting to understand consumer behaviours and the impact this style of service is having on the overall happiness level of the customer.

The research paper, 'The effect of self-checkout quality on customer satisfaction and repatronage in a retail context', explains that there are five attributes that a customer uses to evaluate self-service technology:

1. Speed of service delivery.
2. Perceived control.
3. Reliability.
4. Ease of use.
5. Enjoyment.

In general, happy adopters of self-service transactions are generally young and well-educated, with limited need for personal contact. They are people who consider technology as a source of fun and a novelty. But what if you don't fall into this bracket? Think of the vast number of customers for which this is alienating. (Myself included. I don't go to a supermarket to do more work after a long day.)

According to the same research paper, many consumers still view customer service as a social experience. They value interpersonal interactions and still prefer to deal with people.

Recent studies have shown that our customers' need for human interaction is one of the main reasons they don't like to adopt self-service transactions.

Engage the brain

Well-known author Daniel Goleman has dedicated his life to the science of human relationships. In his book *Social Intelligence* he discusses results from neuro-sociology to explain how sociable our brains are. According to Goleman, we are drawn to other people's brains whenever we engage with another person.

The human need for meaningful connectivity with others, in order to deepen our relationships, is what we all crave, and yet there are countless articles and studies suggesting that we are lonelier than we ever have been and loneliness is now a world health epidemic.

Specifically, in Australia, according to a national Lifeline survey, more than 80% of those surveyed believe our society is becoming a lonelier place. Yet, our brains crave human interaction.

Around a century ago – and still relevant today – the American philosopher and educational reformer John Dewey said that "the deepest urge in human nature is the desire to be important". We need to consider this if we are to become an unsung hero of customer service.

CONNECTION WITHOUT COMPROMISE

As well as speed, efficiency and consistency, there is a less tangible measure that we talk about and critique when we are served as customers: the emotions that we experience with an employee in the moment of service.

Consider the inherent power of the service provider in their relationship with the customer:

- An employee will make a customer feel important or will not.
- An employee will make an interaction feel personal or will not.

- An employee will be 100% attentive to the customer or will not.
- An employee will give meaning to the customer's purchase or will not.
- An employee will allow the customer to feel connected to your brand or will not.

How a customer feels when they interact with your brand relies on how your employee makes them feel, while serving them at the frontline.

Yes, customers can feel a connection to your brand by watching a great video in store or on your website, or experience your brand when they taste your products; however, it is *how they are treated* that lingers long after this. Humans have the unique capability, unlike any robot or automated solution, to provide an interpersonal interaction that creates the social bond that we all look for when seeking connection.

Executive teams, regional managers, even store managers are once, twice or three times removed from the customer and will not have the direct impact that a frontline employee will. Therefore, those employees working closest to your customer are the ones you need to value the most.

The real challenge for future leaders is to, therefore, embrace technology and automation without compromising emotions and customer relationships.

LOYALTY IS A FEELING

The best customer experiences I have had in my life, the most positive and memorable interactions with any brand, have always been the unexpected moments that made me feel special as a customer. The moments that were delivered by a human, not a kiosk touch pad.

How a customer feels about an interaction is the most significant driver of customer loyalty.

According to research done by Bain & Company (the inventor of the Net Promoter Score), increasing your customer retention rates (aka loyalty) by even just 5% will increase profits by 25% to 95%.

The Net Promoter® Score, commonly referred to as NPS®, is a very important customer loyalty metric that gauges how willing a customer is to recommend a product or service. It is used universally by all types of businesses in a cross-section of industries and provides a snapshot in a moment of time for how local customers feel towards a brand based on their service experience.

Our economic value as humans in the retail revolution of AI and robotics has increased. Sure, technology can eliminate jobs, but it is also inspiring us to hold on ever tighter to human values and human ethics.

David Autor, a leading American economist, consistently states in his talks and publications that it is our unique skills and human capabilities that cannot (yet) be replicated or substituted by AI robotics. For instance, humans still have the edge when it comes to things like:

- complex problem solving, that relies on expertise, inductive reasoning or communication skills
- interpersonal interactions and situational adaptability, particularly in more manual roles
- cognitively demanding jobs
- multiplicity of skills
- intuitive mastery.

So having feelings and knowing how to act when experiencing those feelings is our human gift.

AUSTRALIA – THE LUCKY COUNTRY?

When travelling through Greece in 2017 with my partner, every petrol station we stopped at had a well-presented employee who bounced out of their shop, ready to anticipate our needs as they filled up the petrol tank. Every single employee, regardless of who they worked for or whether they were based in inner city or regional areas, cleaned our windscreen.

In a country like Australia, the tradition of filling the tank and cleaning the windscreen of someone's car has long since become extinct. In actual fact, it has become such a rare service component of a petrol station that I think it would freak out my five-year-old niece if she witnessed a stranger approaching our window.

We are missing the opportunity to create a connection with another person through casual banter. Putting a smile on a customer's face is no longer in the job description of a petrol station attendant, nor that of many customer service staff. More importantly, we no longer expect this as customers.

In general, throughout the world, Australia is known as 'the lucky country', with people who are welcoming in nature – yet we struggle most with customer service.

According to a data-driven insights report, *Global Customer Service Barometer*, from American Express, 32% of consumers in Australia believe that companies usually "miss their expectations". Does this really sound that lucky?

So why are we falling short when it comes to good customer service?

LABOUR COSTS CONNECTIONS

A commonality among most organisations in Australia is that labour costs. At the time of publishing this book, SBS reported that Australia was still paying the highest minimum wage compared with countries such as the United Kingdom, America, Canada and Germany, indicating that local wages are out of line with the rest of the world.

Over the decade from 2002, unit labour costs rose 37% in Australia, compared with 29% in Canada, 21% in the US and Korea, 6% in Germany and 16% in Japan.

*We view people in our business as a cost
rather than an asset.*

What you need to see is that human capital is just that: a capital investment in your organisation and your brand. When we yield better actions from our employees we will yield better results in our business. That means we must learn to leverage our service staff, to invest in their development and performance so they want to come to work and give 100% attention to our customers' needs.

The US business empire, Apple, has been doing this for years. It is common to walk past an Apple superstore and see a sea of helpful tech gurus in uniform t-shirts all conversing with a large volume of customers, being friendly, helpful and accessible. Behind the scenes, employees are indoctrinated not inducted. Their training lasts from a few days to up to a few weeks. According to a *Business Insider* article:

> The phrase that trainees hear time and again, which echoes once they arrive at the stores, is "enriching people's lives." The idea is to instil in employees the notion that they are doing something far grander than just selling or fixing products. If there is a secret to Apple's sauce, this is it: the company ennobles employees. It understands that a lot of people will forgo money if they have a sense of higher purpose.

Yet look what happened when one of Australia's largest supermarkets, Coles, tried to embed a more elaborate etiquette in engaging with customers by launching a campaign for Easter 2017 called 'I'm Free', to advertise that they would have more face-to-face service operators open over the busy trading period so you wouldn't have to queue for an automated checkout kiosk. The nation was not only surprised that Coles was competing on service, not the stock-standard price, but outraged due to the campaign's 'flirtatious undertones'. Perhaps they needed to take a leaf out of Apple's training notes.

Competing on price will ramp up more and more thanks to the arrival of Amazon in Australia in 2017. Amazon will continue to squeeze retail margins that will be very hard to beat. It seems a sure bet that competing on service will become increasingly important here to stand out from the competition.

We are so conditioned to poor service that any organisation that shifts the dial in its service will rise to the top of its customers' loyalty list.

CUMULATIVE VERSUS COMPETITIVE

For workforces that have multiple employees spread out across various locations (many of you), one consistent weak link in your chain will eventually add up to poor brand reputation overall.

This works like the butterfly effect. If you're not familiar with this, it comes from the chaos theory of mathematics. It describes what might happen if a butterfly were to brush its wings against the air, just a few inches above the ocean water – eventually creating a massive tidal wave of destruction.

The good news is that the butterfly effect can also have the opposite, positive, effect.

Small daily acts of kindness from your employees, over a long period of time, can create a tidal wave of loyal customers.

These daily acts of devotion need to be delivered by your front-line employees, led by you as leaders. It's imperative that you aspire to have a *cumulative* advantage over a *competitive* one.

A **competitive advantage** involves targeting a type of consumer and making them want to repeat their purchase over time, matching the value proposition to their needs. The value proposition is defined by ensuring there is the right product at a competitive price on offer and it is easy doing business with you. When you do this, your business stays ahead of your competitors and sustains a competitive advantage.

A **cumulative advantage,** on the other hand, involves an emotional connection that a customer has with your brand when they purchase from you. This builds a stronger link between customer and brand. This means your business will be the first that comes to mind for the customer, and they will feel the strongest pull towards your brand, when they are deciding on who to purchase from.

This is less about getting rapid growth and advancing your business, and more about learning to thrive, to increase your company's performance by obsessing about the customer journey at every single interaction, one customer at a time.

This is how you increase customer trust, improve customer loyalty and ultimately drive the performance of your business towards more sustainable long-term growth.

CREATE A CUSTOMER ADVANTAGE

A cumulative customer advantage comprises three things:

1. **Ownership** at all levels of the business, from CEO to frontline employee. No one department or leader owns the customer.
2. **Alignment** to your specific business goals, the economic climate and the environment of your business. There is no point in trying to be something to customers that has no relevance.
3. **Engagement** of employees and their individual performance at work. When employees are engaged, their performance is what has the greatest impact on the customers' feeling towards a brand.

A cumulative customer advantage can only be realised when a service mindset has been cultivated. You must commit to looking at yourself and your people first.

You need to have a cumulative advantage if you have:

- large workforces spread out across multiple locations
- systems and processes in place that need quality consistency across multiple touchpoints
- employees who deliver experiences to customers each day.

When your business has achieved a cumulative customer advantage then you have:

- leaders who are skilled to positively influence the workforce on a daily basis
- customers who feel connected to a brand, which creates a lifetime value
- revenue and profit margins increasing at a sustainable rate.

That's what we all want, right?

Become a business romantic

I was privileged to spend some time with the fabulous Tim Leberecht, author of *The Business Romantic* and a member of the World Economic Forum's Global Agenda Council. Tim and I share the same belief about the beautiful moments that humans can create that robots never will.

Tim says that although humans are complicated and difficult to manage, we have the ability to do the unnecessary. And it's the unnecessary in business that is necessary. He believes that the romance in business has been lost and it's the humans in businesses – consumer or producer, employee or entrepreneur – who can do things like catch us off guard, create something from nothing and add completely unnecessary steps into an interaction that he defines as beautiful.

So now is the time for us to tune in to our emotions in the workplace more than ever and create more 'beautiful' among the automated 'expected'. What an opportunity we all have with this human gift: the ability to read emotions.

Speed of service is easy to measure and easy to manage but it doesn't tell you accurately how well customers are being treated and, more importantly, how they feel.

2

Conscious leaders drive a service culture

If you want to change the world, start with yourself.

MAHATMA GANDHI

Some people say he was a bully, others say persistent, whereas I would call him a master. With a clear vision and a good dose of tenacity, Ray Kroc built the $700-million-per-annum fast food revolution that is McDonald's. His secret to building the empire that now feeds 1% of the world's population (as quoted at the end of *The Founder* movie)? Employ the right people and teach them the systems later.

While most people suggest operational systems and automating is what made the brand a global giant, and the poster child for any franchise, it was recently revealed in the 2016 Hollywood blockbuster *The Founder* that it was actually the type of employee that the golden arches attracted, and Kroc's obsession with building a tribe of brand advocates, that was the trick.

Kroc's ideal franchisees were young families who had gumption and a desire to create a real sense of place in a great restaurant. They were willing to roll up their sleeves and hustle. Once recruited, they then adopted the strict processes and procedures which are directly responsible for the company's significant growth, from 1954 to today.

More than 60 years on, McDonald's is one of the largest real estate holders in the world and is a shining example of a company that has achieved a successful customer service culture.

McDonald's created a cumulative advantage, while also maintaining consistency across all the various customer touchpoints: service, quality, cleanliness and value. The McDonald's formula means that no matter where you might buy a cheeseburger in the world, it would still taste like a cheeseburger.

The organisation is also consistently committed to the growth and development of its people. Career progression in McDonald's was, and still is, a serious part of its business. When I worked at McDonald's in the regional town of Port Macquarie, I was responsible for more than $100,000 weekly revenue, I knew how it felt to run a team during a $2,000 hour – and I was just 19!

It is no accident that McDonald's employees, particularly those who have held leadership positions, stand out on resumes compared to other potential candidates. They have been part of a culture that understands service. They have been trained and developed in an environment that treats its employees, and its leaders, as being just as important as its customers.

When your leaders feel invested in, cared for, and know their potential, or how far they can grow in a business, they are not only engaged in what they are doing, but inspired to do more.

Nurture the vital few

The 80/20 rule (Pareto principle) is derived from Italian economist Vilfredo Pareto who created a mathematical formula based on an observation that only a "vital few" of the peapods in his garden produced the majority of peas. Originally, the Pareto principle referred to the observation that 80% of Italy's wealth belonged to only 20% of the population.

Some other examples of the Pareto principle playing out in society include:

- 20% of criminals commit 80% of crimes
- 20% of drivers cause 80% of all traffic accidents
- 80% of pollution originates from 20% of all factories
- 20% of a company's products represent 80% of sales
- 20% of employees are responsible for 80% of the results
- 20% of students have grades 80% or higher.

In business, we would say that 20% of the inputs or activities are responsible for 80% of the outcomes or results.

So when it comes to service, you and your team are "the vital few" in the garden that need to be nurtured. This is where 80% of your company's efforts will come from in shifting the dial towards a culture of a service mindset.

SET THE TONE

Leadership is about being consistent. It's about consistently behaving and showing up how are you 'showing up' as a role model that others respect. Whether you realise it or not, you set the tone for the day, the shift, that moment with each and every one of your interactions with your employees. In turn, this has a flow-on effect on your customers.

If I were to ask you to think of one person who has had the greatest impact in helping you become the person you are today, who would that be for you?

Your reasons for choosing that one person may be largely due to the way they behaved, how they helped you see something you could not see, how they supported you and were committed to developing you at a time when you needed it. Whatever the reason is, it was impactful and important enough for you to remember.

So what if you were that person for someone else? For your teams and for your customers?

We cannot possibly know just how much we affect our teams and the culture of our business from our every mood, every thought, every gesture, every word.

You set the tone of your culture, the expectation of your employees and of the type of service your customers receive.

MAKE IT STICK

All organisations want service programs and any level of investment in people to be long-lasting and sticky. When training and development is seen in a business as being a valuable activity, it is usually because it has not dissolved after a few months of the initial hype, but rather the initiatives have created a step change and the service behaviours have stuck.

The methodology I use that achieves the stickiest results when creating a customer service mindset is developing frontline leaders.

Figure 2.1 below shows which of the employees of our Unsung Hero, Hudsons Coffee from the Emirates Leisure Retail Australia (ELRA), have the closest connections to their customers. (To read more about Hudsons Coffee, one of the six companies profiled in this book as Unsung Heroes because of their exceptional approach to customer service, go to page 128.)

Figure 2.1: Customer connections, ELRA

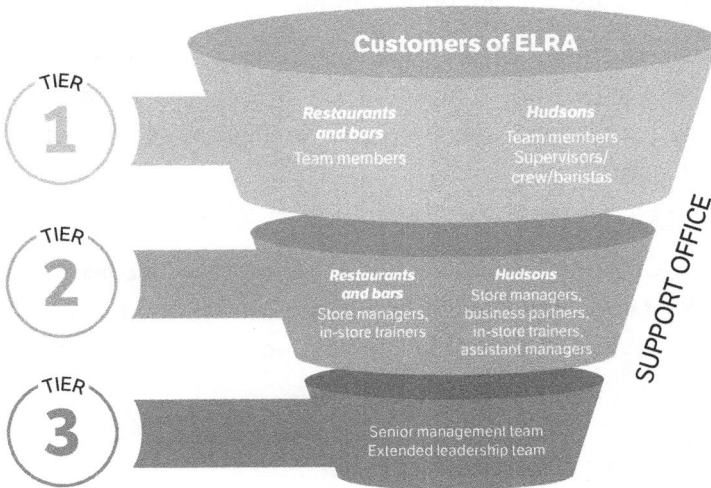

This inverted pyramid (I call it the funnel) was inspired by a philosophy in the book *The Nordstrom Way to Customer Service Excellence*. Its intention is to remind people that customers are always at the top, the number one priority, and the employees closest to the customer are those we should value the most.

The most valuable people in your workforce are the frontline employees (tier 1), those closest to the customer who have direct contact with them every single day. The frontline leaders (tier 2) are not closest to the customer all day, however they are most certainly closest to the frontline teams every single day, and that counts.

If you want strength in your frontline employees when it comes to delivering exceptional service, then the deliberate, daily focus must come from the tier 2 level managers. It will be your efforts, as a frontline leader, which will have the greatest impact in shifting the dial positively towards a long-lasting service mindset in your organisation.

The perfect approach for creating a customer service mindset across a large workforce would also include the senior leaders and executive teams (tier 3), as well as any support office employees.

Consistent quality service experiences will be the slight edge that your customers are looking for, and that necessitates having your whole organisation onboard.

BECOME A CONSCIOUS LEADER

As service leaders in a hierarchical organisation, you are directly responsible for the frontline workforce, so it is up to you to cultivate a service culture. You need to be the Ray Kroc of your industry. You need to promote, encourage and lead your frontline staff, so that they in turn will look after and nurture your most valuable assets – your customers.

The health of your service culture is determined by the health of its individual members. This starts with you as a frontline leader. It's a universal law that the energy you bring will be the energy others bring.

As Confucius says:

> When the father is a father and the son a son,
> when the brother is a brother and the sister a sister,
> when the husband is a husband and the wife a wife,
> then the family is set in order.
> When the family is set in order, the village is set in order.
> When the village is set in order, the nation is set in order.
> When the nation is set in order, the world is set in order.

To truly operate your organisation with a cumulative advantage, you need to become a conscious frontline leader, as shown in Figure 2.2.

Figure 2.2: The conscious frontline leader

Leader type	Behaviour	Individual impact	Network impact	Employee performance	Customer impact
Conscious	Influencing	Effortless	Cumulative advantage	↑20%	Trust
Motivating	Engaging	Energised	Competitive advantage	↑10%	Differentiated
Informing	Supervising	Exhausted	Compliant	↓5%	Satisfaction
Functioning	Transacting	Effort	Disengaged	↓10%	Service
Missing	Disengaged	Existing	Damaging	↓20%	Dissatisfaction

Let's explore each section of the model in more detail. As you read, make some time for self-reflection and see if you can assess where you are at now and, more importantly, where you want to be.

Missing leader

If you're a missing leader then you are either literally never to be found or are very good at being busy. (I am not sure what is worse!)

You are disengaged from the organisation and can be extremely damaging in an intense people environment where social interactions matter and relationships need to be formed. How often are you focusing on things that are in your urgent pile versus things that are important, ie deepening your relationships with your team?

The damage caused by a missing leader includes high staff turnover, which makes it very difficult for customers to form familiar or loyal relationships with your employees and your brand.

Functioning leader

If you're functioning then you are getting the job done in a transactional way.

You have the technical know-how, are consistently compliant and ticking the boxes that relate to quality, speed and efficiencies, and it's likely you were promoted because you could perform the tasks the best. You are failing to delegate, to empower and motivate your staff.

The impact this has on your workforce is a general feeling of disconnection with the team and a lack of trust. A functioning leader defines success as seeing staff 'getting the job done' and does not see the value in creating rapport and relationships internally, let alone with customers.

How often do you feel you need to repeat yourself and can never really trust your team to do the work without you? Now ask, what would happen if one day they did do the work without you?

Learning to recognise staff in your team for the value they bring through their behaviours and attitudes is the key to your leadership and will move you higher up the ladder.

Informing leader

If you're informing then you are supervising your staff, telling them what to do without encouraging them to provide input themselves and learn. This means you are often exhausted because you're working extremely hard *in* the business and not *on* the business. Your staff are also just going through the motions, doing their job because they have been told to, not because they understand why or how they are adding value to a greater, collective purpose.

When a customer is on the receiving end of an employee who is task focused, there is little room left for personality, conversation and human-to-human connection to shine through, which results in ordinary experiences, with no real point of difference to the competitor down the road.

When you start to ask questions of your employees, when you show instead of tell, then you will start to move towards a place of motivation.

Motivating leader

A motivating leader is capable of getting great results and energising a tribe of employees to channel their focus and energy into the right place. You impact your team well and keep their spirits high in times of uncertainty or when under pressure. But how long can this motivation last?

Leaders cannot be everywhere all the time and so their efforts may not be as long-lasting when they are not around. This has a flow-on effect on your customers. You risk service experiences that are a little hit-and-miss, particularly if an employee is having a bad day. Motivation alone is not enough for frontline staff to stay switched on for several hours a day.

Conscious leader

A conscious leader is present and mindful throughout the day. You have a reputation for being incredibly influential and can get the best out of your team in an effortless way. You spend the majority of your day with the people who matter, those that are closest to your customers.

You ask great questions of your staff, you listen deeply, you see things through others' eyes and always explain clearly the intention behind things. You are rarely frantic or stressed and through your own daily habits and behaviours, you gain trust from your employees, which creates a truly influential tribe.

You now have a workforce that is consistently engaged, performing at their optimum level and supporting each other to make sure that the small daily acts of devotion to your customers are felt regardless of the time of day, purchase price or length of transaction.

Our job as leaders is to encourage our teams to love giving service, and to do that we need to become conscious.

SET YOUR FOUNDATIONS

As we just explored, a conscious service leader is focused on *being* a leader and looking after the people in the business, rather than *doing* all the task-orientated business stuff. Sounds good, right?

Like a house, you must have strong foundations to keep you from collapsing and to enable you to foster trust in those around you.

There are three foundational pillars that make up a conscious leader, as shown in Figure 2.3 and discussed below.

Figure 2.3: The conscious service leader

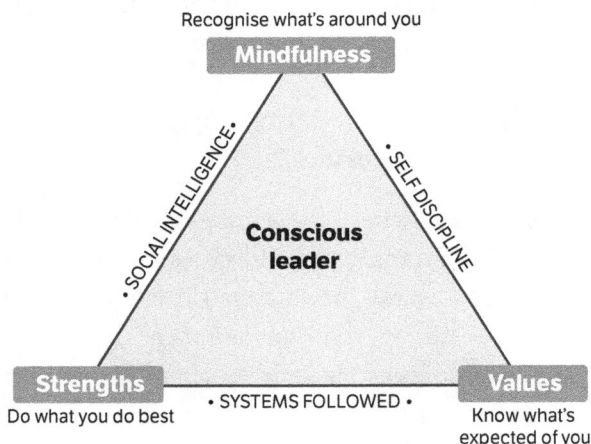

1. Strengths – do what you do best

Many service leaders are good at many things; however, most are truly great at a small set of important and unique skills. We will call these unique skills 'strengths'.

When we are working with our strengths, we often feel good. They are not just things that we do well, but also things that we look forward to doing; they energise us and excite us. Using our strengths seems second nature or automatic. This is especially true in a robust service environment, where our strengths enable us to perform at our best and under pressure.

When you spend your time using the few strengths you have, you become an exceptional leader and colleague for everyone you interact with.

The benefits of understanding your strengths include:

- supporting your wellbeing (mental health, stress levels, physical health, satisfaction with life)
- boosting your performance (greater confidence, gains in growth and development, job performance and job meaning)
- improving the bottom line (lifting employee engagement, optimising team performance).

One of the tools I use to help clients identify strengths is Your Personal Character Strengths Profile, created by psychologists Dr Martin Seligman and the late Dr Christopher Peterson. There is a free survey that anyone can undertake that gives you a full summary of your 24 character strengths at www.viacharacter.org.

Otherwise, I have also found the Gallup CliftonStrengths assessment a very easy and relevant tool for the workplace. You can complete a survey for a small fee at www.gallup-strengthscentre.com.

2. Mindfulness – recognise what's around you

In the service industry, when leaders must perform for hours at a time, it is particularly challenging to be mindful in every situation. Our minds are busy at the best of times, but there always seems to be another voice in our head making comments, judging, criticising and rationalising when we are doing a task or speaking with someone.

When we are mindless, we miss many verbal and non-verbal clues that can assist us in making better decisions with our team and in decisions that impact our customers. Mindlessness is a huge contributor to misunderstandings and missed opportunities.

Mindfulness, on the other hand, helps our interpersonal relationships. When we are mindful we take control of what we focus on, we control our attention, we self-regulate. We are calmer in our approach when things feel out of our control. We have greater empathy for our clients, our customers and our employees, which leads to clearer communication, better relationships and trust.

Becoming more mindful can be as simple as taking in a breath and consciously noticing our body language, facial expressions, tone of voice and what is not being said or done.

When we are more mindful, our team members will notice this too. The quality of conversations and interactions will lift, which will have a flow-on effect on our customers.

Five Senses

There are many books, applications, podcasts and resources to help you to become more mindful, but I like this one for a busy service environment or workplace.

1. **Notice five things you can see.** Pick something that you don't usually notice, like a shadow or a small crack in the concrete.

2. **Notice four things you can feel.** Bring awareness to four things you are currently feeling, like the texture of your trousers or the feeling of a breeze on your skin.

3. **Notice three things you can hear.** Take a moment to listen to and note three things that you can hear in the background. This could be the hum of a refrigerator, the faint sound of traffic nearby or birds chirping.

4. **Notice two things you can smell.** Bring your awareness to smells you usually filter out, whether they're pleasant or unpleasant.

5. **Notice one thing you can taste.** Focus on one thing you can taste right now, in this moment. You can take a sip of drink, chew a piece of gum, eat something or just notice the current taste in your mouth or open your mouth to search the air for a taste.

Practise this the next time you are entering a conversation with a team member or in a break between activities or meetings. You could also encourage your staff to practise this in between serving customers.

3. Values – know what's expected of you

I find leaders can establish quicker commonalities among their staff if the organisation has defined values. You must know what your organisation sees as being important and ultimately what it believes in.

Values allow people to know where they stand and can act as a barometer for making decisions with confidence. Overall, when values are visible and embedded into the organisational culture, the environment feels like a safe place in which to speak up and contribute and everyone seems to accept each other more on an equal level regardless of the organisational hierarchy.

If you have no clear organisational values, it can take longer to collaborate and see things from each other's point of view. There is much confusion around what 'good' looks like and it is obvious that it looks different for everyone, leading to greater risk of inconsistency. There is more judgement and defensiveness as people's opinions hold greater weight in the absence of any set values. There are too many different things to focus on when trying to engage staff and improve performance.

Customers are no longer just interested in the value that you deliver; they are also interested in the values that you hold as an organisation.

Remember, you are responsible for setting the tone of a culture and therefore the way you live and model the values of an organisation, or if not – your behaviours will determine the actions and reactions of your employees on the frontline.

Your behaviours need to be driven by the organisation's values, and show employees what's expected from them in their performance.

Consider your actions and behaviours at work.
How are your actions and reactions influencing the
environment around you?

What happens if you work for an organisation and there are no values set in place? And therefore, there are no clearly defined behaviours being demonstrated?

First, what a wonderful opportunity this is! It would be a great conversation starter to find out from key personnel why there are no defined values of the organisation.

Next, when you lead a store, a shop or a team yourself, the team have potentially determined their own culture and perhaps this is where you could start to develop organisational values.

Ideally, having a common set of values across a whole organisation where there are multiple stores, seen through service behaviours, will achieve greater consistency of quality service. However, in the absence of any company values, set some yourself as a mini 'satellite' culture.

Here are some useful pointers when setting values:

1. Decide on them collaboratively with your team.
2. Make sure the words chosen to express your values are verbs. You want them to be 'doing' words.
3. List key behaviours of what the value looks like in action. This is how to bring the values to life.

4. Communicate them to the team, celebrate them and ask for clarity from your team members on how they see these values being lived out in their own roles.
5. Refer to them daily when recognising good behaviours and making decisions.

You will be surprised how much of a positive impact the process of deciding on values will have on your organisation if executed correctly. We are, at the end of the day, creatures who crave social bonds and connections. Values connect people.

EXERCISE RIGHT

To lead a successful service culture, you must become a conscious leader and that means exercising right: mentally, physically and emotionally.

Being a conscious leader means you practise leading consistently. This means that a lot of what we are about to talk about does not come naturally to some of us, and we may need to consider developing new mindsets and 'rewiring' our behaviours. This requires commitment and practice if you want to make any change.

Through commitment and practice you can learn to be a conscious leader.

Do a quick check-in now. Do you avoid:

- Serving people yourself?
- Trying to understand your employees?
- Having difficult conversations with employees?

- Asking staff for solutions and ideas?
- Using tools to help show what good service looks like?
- Talking feelings and instead just talk facts?
- Connecting people to something greater than the task at hand?
- Practising being a better leader?

If you answered 'yes' to any of the questions above, the great news is that this book will help you see the benefit of moving towards some new behaviours and practices that are not additional work, just different. Avoidance and disengagement, such as in the examples listed above, only move you further away from your highest potential as a leader – and deep down I know you want to do the best work you possibly can and live a life you are proud of.

It is much easier to learn systems and procedures.
It is more difficult to learn attitudes and behaviours.

There's no denying it – being a conscious leader is challenging. But rising to challenges will make you better at what you do and will give you a richer understanding of the people you work with and for.

PART II

THE SIX SERVICE MINDSETS

As we've just explored, we tend to overcomplicate so much of service. We get set in our own ways, stay in our own heads and forget that we are simply serving humans with our product or service. We try to control what happens in a service environment, which as you well know isn't possible!

So the best, simplest and easiest way of developing a successful service culture is to work on your service mindset. This is a continuum of behaviours that you, as a leader, adopt. Your behaviours impact your employees' performance, which in turn impacts your customer interactions and loyalty, creating a virtuous circle that enhances your whole organisation.

In-depth consideration of how your employees experience your organisation in the workplace, and how they feel about this, is the shift in mindset required to enhance customer experience. As Diane Gherson, IBM's Chief Human Resources Officer, puts it:

> We've found that employee engagement explains two-thirds of our client experience scores. And if we're able to increase client satisfaction by five points on an account, we see an extra 20% revenue, on average.

THE SIX SERVICE MINDSETS

We will be focusing on the following six service mindsets:

1. **Empathy** – Leaders who practise empathy create a team of employees who feel understood. Cultivating trust in this way is essential for frontline leaders who have teams that are continually coaching, mentoring, teaching and caring for others.

2. **Questions** – These are a way of showing sincere interest in your employees as humans to help them grow into their role, and to help them facilitate the needs of your customers. When you ask the right questions, you are encouraging your staff to think for themselves and learn the effect of their decisions.

3. **Energy** – What you give attention to grows. Therefore, leaders looking for best practice in their teams need to immediately shift the focus, the energy, onto supporting all employees to deliver great service.

4. **Heart** – When your staff feel that you trust them and appreciate them, they have a greater willingness to serve, which automatically increases their discretionary effort. Having a workforce of willing employees gives greater consistency across all customer interaction and creates a cumulative advantage for an organisation.

5. **Purpose** – Leaders who help staff see they are an important part of the whole success journey make staff feel valued, which motivates them further. An engaged workforce interacts with your customers more positively and this creates customer loyalty.

6. **Practice** – Being a leader involves conscious practise of behaviours and attitudes such as continually seeking information, developing people and helping people grow themselves in their working roles. Knowing that you are only as good as your last performance is key to continual growth and improvement and business longevity.

THE UNSUNG HEROES

Leaders are instrumental in shifting the culture of an organisation, but they are not often recognised for their efforts or results. More often than not, they remain Sherpas in the shadows – until now.

To help you understand the importance of each of the six mindsets, each of the mindset chapters will finish with a case study of an Australian organisation that has created outstanding customer service by developing that particular mindset. I call these organisations Unsung Heroes. They just keep going about their business, giving clients and customers top customer service, because they have adopted the right mindsets.

Of course, each of the Unsung Heroes is led by teams of conscious leaders. The Unsung Heroes may not get as much street cred or exposure as Google, Amazon or Facebook, but they are leading the way when it comes to delivering superior customer service in the world. You'll get inside insight into the real and tangible activities, processes and mindsets these organisations and their leaders have adopted to gain customer loyalty and longevity. Not only that, but you'll see the data that backs up the evidence.

Some of the Unsung Heroes have been measured internally or externally through Qualtrics (www.qualtrics.com/au), the customer service industry's leading experience management company and software. More than 7,000 enterprises worldwide, including half of the Fortune 100 and 99 of the top 100 business schools, rely on Qualtrics technology.

You'll soon see that to make it as an Unsung Hero your most powerful and influential weapon in your business is not a complex set of service standards, but the simple and effortless behaviours that you and your teams use every day, naturally, human to human.

Their success is simple to follow. So your organisation can become an Unsung Hero too.

Mindset 1: Empathy

Never criticize a man until you've walked a mile in his moccasins

AMERICAN INDIAN PROVERB

It was my first day working as an executive in a new not-for-profit organisation. I was nervous, excited and determined. This was a big gig for me. Leading up to this day I already had a sense that most people who worked for this brand were emotionally connected to the organisation's purpose, and most were so passionate about working there that they said it was their dream job.

I remember my first meeting with the CEO like it was yesterday. I proudly presented my first 90-day plan and talked through a sophisticated model on how I was going to approach the challenge he had set for me.

I was so determined and focused on the results, doing the work, that I allowed this 'doing' mindset to seep into my approach when forming new relationships with people, in meetings and one-on-one interactions. I was so focused on having an impact that I came across to everyone else in my team as someone who did not have a good understanding of the business, did not acknowledge their problems and was unable to put themselves in others' shoes.

I didn't show enough interest in the things that people were interested in, the very reason they were there in the first place.

The impact that this had on my ability to develop trust with key people was detrimental. In fact, it set me back 90 days, not forwards. Even once I reset my focus to form relationships, my authenticity was questioned – it was too late. That is why empathy is the first leadership behaviour you need to develop to inspire a high-performing workforce.

You've got to focus on forming relationships first:
that's how you get the results later.

ARE YOU BLIND?

The business world would have you believe that a leader is someone who is strong, defiant, has all the answers and never ever shows emotion or makes time to 'get to know people'. Emotion is seen as a no-no. We couldn't be getting this more wrong!

Getting your inbox to zero and crossing things off your to-do list does not make you a great leader. When we focus heavily on these type of activities, we create blind spots and make bad decisions.

Building strong relationships at work is critical to being an effective leader. When we display empathy with our employees, we have a far greater chance of building rapport and the person on the receiving end of your interaction starts to feel that you genuinely care about them.

Having the ability to walk in someone else's shoes and see the world through their eyes is crucial to customer service and to building trust.

Trust in yourself

Building trust is just as important internally within the workplace culture as it is with the consumer, explains Rob Lorimer, Executive Manager responsible for the Customer Experience Program at Commonwealth Scientific and Industrial Research Organisation (CSIRO).

"Our employee surveys tell us that the level of trust between our people is really high. The foundations here are very strong," Rob says.

"They trust each other's technical expertise and all feel that they are part of something much bigger than themselves, that there is meaning and real purpose to what they are doing here at CSIRO. We understand each other's commonalities and if we do not, we seek to understand; the camaraderie forms and trust is a key outcome from this."

"When we come together and meet we are often being collegial. We have a workforce here that in the main are scientists and they have the ability to get in a room and actually reach consensus on things. Everyone gets on very well, it's needed."

EMPATHY, NOT SYMPATHY

Remember *Beauty and the Beast*, where Belle, despite her fears, learns to look beyond the Beast's exterior and discover his kind heart? Or *The BFG*, where Sophie learns, through asking questions, that in fact the giant is gentle and charming? And of course, *E.T.*, the story of a little boy who welcomed an extra-terrestrial into his home and becomes so connected with it, he starts to take on its feelings?

From a young age, these classics have taught us to avoid judgement, ask questions and always try to see the world from others' points of view. They have also taught us the difference between *sympathy* and *empathy*.

For example, in *E.T.*, Elliot helps plan the alien's escape with a team of mates. He is driven by a deep understanding that E.T. wants to go home. Despite the risks and dangers of coordinating such a mission, the young boy steps up to the plate as a leader and conducts himself from a place of kindness and understanding. He treats E.T. how he would wish to be treated.

If, however, Elliot had been sympathetic to E.T.'s plight then he probably wouldn't have been driven to act! Sure, he would have shown compassion, but probably felt useless as a result.

Often leaders and employees get sympathy and empathy confused, especially when dealing with customer complaints. Customers want an apology but more importantly they want their issue fixed. Showing pity or compassion for a customer, but not getting on with solving the problem, is counterproductive in building trust in relationships, and yet this is what many of us do.

Daniel Pink sums empathy up beautifully in his book, *A Whole New Mind*:

> Empathy is about standing in someone else's shoes, feeling with his or her heart and seeing with his or her eyes. Not only is empathy hard to outsource, it makes the world a better place.

Empathy is one of the most effective ways of connecting human to human and that's why it's so crucial in a service culture.

Research suggests human interaction is the primary way people judge service quality. These are the interactions that shape your organisation's reputation, by a customer determining whether or not they are satisfied.

The paper 'Factors of Customer Satisfaction on Services' shows that customer satisfaction happens when we approach our work with a belief that each customer deserves our focused attention and kindness. This in turn builds trust and loyalty which can only be created when we take time to observe, ask questions and respond thoughtfully to the people we serve, ensuring that we are meeting their needs.

Empathy cultivates trust and is essential for frontline leaders who are continually coaching, mentoring, teaching and caring for others.

THREE TYPES OF EMPATHY

According to Daniel Goleman, psychologist and leading thinker in the areas of emotional intelligence and social intelligence, there are three kinds of empathy:

1. **Cognitive empathy** – the ability to understand another's point of view.
2. **Emotional empathy** – the ability to feel what someone else feels.
3. **Empathic concern** – the ability to sense what another person needs from you.

Cultivating all three kinds of empathy, which originate in different parts of the brain, is important for building social relationships.

Of the three, the first one – cognitive empathy – is the most important for frontline leaders to develop. You need to be able to listen to your employees attentively, to understand their point of view and show them how to practise this – focusing their attention out, to understand the customer's point of view – when serving customers.

When you develop cognitive empathy you:

- read people's moods or non-verbal cues accurately
- take an active interest in people's concerns
- listen attentively to understand another person's point of view
- understand others' perspectives when they are different from your own
- understand the reasons for another person's actions.

The most powerful ability that you have when influencing and inspiring your staff is the ability to form trust.

SHALLOW VERSUS RAPID

Think of a situation where you met someone for the first time in a social setting. How deep did you go in the conversation versus how shallow was the chit-chat? How quickly did you establish rapport, where you felt at ease and some trust began to build?

You can feel it. You can tell when an interaction feels fake versus someone who is genuinely focused on you. When a 'shallow disconnect' occurs (see below for some examples of this), often someone is stuck in their own head and making the conversation all about them. The questions they ask you do not make you feel like they are genuinely interested in you.

When a customer and employee interact, it will be either a shallow disconnect or a rapid rapport scenario. The employee's level of empathic ability will determine the quality of the interaction.

You have to learn to cultivate rapid rapport with your staff so that they in turn develop that with your customers.

In a *shallow disconnect* situation, the employee is:

- Doing all the talking and no asking.
- Not reading or observing the signals of the customer, and transacts rather than translates.

- Robotic in their response and doesn't attempt to make any personal connection with the human they are interacting with.
- Focused on the task they assume they are completing, and fails to ask questions so as to meet the customer's real needs.

Whereas in a *rapid rapport* situation the employee is:

- Listening deeply to the customer and acknowledging what they are hearing.
- Asking relevant questions in order to better understand the customer's needs.
- Focused on what the customer needs and delivers solutions that are relevant.

Rapid rapport is what we aim for in all service environments. The sooner you start practising this, then the sooner your employees will practise this with your customers.

How a customer feels about an interaction is the most significant driver of customer loyalty.

DEVELOP EMPATHY

There are three things you can do to help you develop more empathy at work so that you can better connect with your employees and so they can better connect with your customers.

1. Make time for reflection
2. Practise deep listening
3. Care more about solutions.

1. Make time for reflection

We all have the capacity to feel emotions but being aware of how they show up, when they show up and how this impacts others is critical in a leadership role.

Every interaction you have with your team has an emotional subtext. When you frown, it makes others worried; when you smile, it makes others feel happy. This is a transfer of feeling called emotional contagion and it's why self-awareness and time for reflection are crucial as a frontline leader.

The great news is that you can check yourself often. You can check yourself at the times of the day that matter the most. Check yourself before your day begins, before you start your shift, before you walk into a meeting.

A great technique that I have used over the years is a quick, quiet Catch, Check and Correct.

- **Catch your thoughts and emotions:** what am I thinking and feeling right now?
- **Check them:** how will these thoughts and emotions serve me and the people around me?
- **Correct them:** what is a more useful way of being in this moment for myself and others?

Unfortunately for most of us, leadership cannot take place while living under a rock. We are exposed, seen and observed. We are human, which means we too have emotions. It is tricky to avoid bringing emotions into an interaction, so greater awareness of them will be helpful. Remember, emotions are contagious. We catch emotions much as we do a virus. Even when people try to suppress all signs of their emotions, feelings have a way of leaking in.

Assess and reassess

Practise the following activity at the end of each week to help you assess your levels of empathy and improve the next time you interact with an employee.

1. List several situations that occurred in the last week during which you communicated a message.
2. Rate each situation on a scale of 1 to 5 depending on how well you believe you communicated the message.
3. List what emotions were reflected and how they were conveyed verbally and non-verbally.
4. List how many times you asked questions and who did most of the talking.
5. List how effective the response was, on a scale of 1 to 5, from your team/employee.
6. Rate how satisfied you were, on a scale of 1 to 5, with the conclusion of the interaction.
7. Identify what you could say or do differently next time to increase your level of satisfaction and your empathy.

2. Practise deep listening

We cannot be empathetic if we do not learn to listen. However, there is a big difference between listening to respond and listening to understand.

Listening to *respond* is really someone wanting to finish your sentence, give you the answer or contribute to the conversation so they feel good, important and heard, which in actual fact makes it all about them and not about you.

Listening to *understand* requires you to have a single-minded focus on what is happening in that very moment. It requires you to avoid tuning into the internal dialogue and chatter of the mind; it requires you to be fully there with attention out to the person in front of you. This is super tricky when we are often serving people (employees and customers) in noisy environments with many distractions like phones and emails.

As leaders, I'm sure we can all relate to a situation in service where we have started a conversation with an employee and they have not heard us. They have been stuck in their own head, possibly made some assumptions about your needs and how the interaction will play out, and as a consequence have missed a cue from you and made the whole interaction feel disingenuous and fake.

Conscious leaders will display brilliant listening skills. Their attention is out towards the other person, they block distractions when with people, they listen to understand, they care, they listen to what is not being said and to context and meaning behind the words.

Staff will always start by telling you what you want to hear or what they think you want to hear. The truth about a matter, or how an employee is feeling, will eventually come out, provided there is enough space and silence for the employee.

The best way to practise listening to understand is to be silent.

Allowing some space for silence in a conversation may initially feel a little uncomfortable and you may get a strange reaction from staff who are used to you doing all the talking, however it is extremely powerful in getting your employees to trust you and speak up.

Maybe you could open a meeting or a topic during a meeting with a question or a statement that you wish to hear your team's views on. Rather than give them some ideas or show them what you are looking for, be quiet. Push through the awkward silence barrier where you may naturally feel you need to fill in the blanks and fill the empty space to get moving so it's a productive meeting.

If you want to further practise deep listening, I highly recommend the work of Oscar Trimboli, a thought leader in this space. I use his activity cards in workshops to help leaders facilitate deep listening.

3. Care more about solutions

I find reviewing complaint handling procedures is a fantastic exercise for leaders to reinforce empathy with their teams. Why? Because most complaints happen when leaders are not available.

As a leader, it is important to let go, not feel you have control of every service interaction and realise that your role is to empower your people. This is a fantastic way to do that.

To give your employees the best possible chance of displaying empathy with a customer, consider approaching empathy (via your complaint handling procedure) in the following ways:

- Review your complaint handling procedure and consider the overarching message for an employee when they are learning the complaint handling process. Are they hearing "Keep apologising" or are they hearing "Get on with fixing the problem with care"?
- Gather a group of employees from your business to discuss complaint handling. Ask them how empowered they feel

to fix problems themselves, what tools they would want access to for them to be more empowered, and what further support they may need from you to make sure that at the end of the day the customer is getting a strong sense that their problem will be resolved.

- Something as simple as encouraging staff to paraphrase and sum up what the next steps are, that they will be doing to help fix the problem, is often all a customer needs to hear to feel satisfied they are in good hands.

Get out of your head and keep your attention outwards. Empathy will keep you humble, build trust with your people and help you transform your approach to your work and your relationships.

Reflecting on empathy

1. When do you build in time to get to know your employees?

2. How do you reflect on your own emotions and the impact they have when you are leading?

3. Think of some examples of service interactions you have seen. Can you begin to identify what empathy looks like in action?

4. What were the results of your end-of-week reflection activity where you assess and reassess your interactions with employees?

5. How would your team describe your listening skills?

6. When did you last review your complaints handling procedure and look at the steps through the eyes of the customer? How quickly do you get to solving the problem?

UNSUNG HERO: VOLKSWAGEN GROUP AUSTRALIA

"Obsess about your employees and customers"

Volkswagen Group Australia (VGA) has a relentless focus on improving customer experience across more than 140 dealerships in Australia, even through troubled times. The mindset that the company has developed best is empathy. We've just discussed empathy in theory. Here is how VGA shows empathy in practice.

In 2015, the German car giant admitted cheating on emissions tests in the US, sending shockwaves throughout the world. To try to regain customer trust and loyalty the organisation worked hard to improve its Net Promoter Score (NPS) by over 25 points in 2017 (within two years). At a national level VGA's performance improved on average by 20% across the key touchpoints directly related to loyalty.

I spent time interviewing Jason Bradshaw, Director Customer Experience, and through these conversations I learned that training and development of its people was a high priority for VGA. Sales skills, technical skills and customer service skills all receive equal effort and investment.

Internal advocacy has been Jason's priority first, in order to build customer advocacy for the group: "Whether it be here in our head office, whether it be with our field team, or whether it be in the dealership."

Jason explained their "obsession and unrelenting, unapologetic... (for want of a better term) in your face agendas", in focusing on the employee experience. He described the multiple touchpoints, such as team roadshows, events and conferences, where they took the opportunity to keep raising the awareness of customer service in the business and keep the importance of service front and centre of everyone's mind. And not only through discussions: "We had to get the balance of people understanding the theory of great service as well as people experiencing it first hand themselves."

Jason reminds us that we need to treat our employees the way we wish our customers to be treated. As he put it:

Be obsessed about your team members' experience at work first and foremost and your customers second.

Jason describes how he tries to wow his employees at regular training summits:

> When we bring our teams together we want them to feel an experience at a level of excellence that we are asking them to create for their own customers back in their dealerships. Their experiences at the hotel, the conference centre, are just as important for us to get right as the content we present and information they learn and take away with them. We want our employees to pay attention to the little things and be impressed with their experience. Our first goal, when bringing dealership owners and leaders together for a few days, is for them to feel and understand for two days what we mean when we talk about a consistent premium experience.

My takeaway from this first insight into VGA's approach to service training is that you really do need to educate your employees on *how* to treat customers. You do this by showing them, by making your employees feel what it is like to be treated as important.

I was curious to know how VGA continued this engagement with their employees once they left the summit and returned to their own dealerships. I was keen to learn what sort of tools and ways of packaging their learnings have been helpful for Jason and the team to get their customer service messages across. When I asked, Jason handed me a small book, *100 Ways to Wow*. He then described the first day he introduced this pocket-sized tool and how it's working for them today:

> It was the first time the managers had met me and I had to get up on the stage and announce what my grand plan was. Our service strategy for the Volkswagen brands is called 'Accelerate to Wow'. We define 'wow' as wanting to impress customers, wanting to build an emotional connection with customers and being, effectively, 1% better than average. But, often, we aim to be 1% better consistently in every touchpoint than our competitors. I think when I mentioned the word 'wow' the first time, people said to me, "We don't use that word in the automotive industry. What does it really mean?" I said, "Let me break it down. When a customer walks out of dealerships or has an interaction with us, however they have an interaction with us, we want them to go and tell their friends and family." If they use the word 'wow', fine, if they use super or whatever... it doesn't matter about the word, it's that actual feeling, that emotional connection they create with the brand because that's what's going to build a lifetime owner and advocate.

The fact that the book contains 101 ways to wow customers just shows how VGA goes above and beyond for its customers. Every dealership received this guide and they were encouraged to take a moment from time to time and remember the little things that really do wow customers. Jason adds:

Tools like our *100 Ways to Wow* help knock down this perception that customer experience is a department. They create the inherent knowledge, in plain language, that every single person in the dealership is responsible for the customer experience.

Wow No. 26 emphasises the empathetic approach VGA employees are encouraged to take:

"Put yourself in the customer's shoes. How would you feel in their situation?"

Volkswagen realises that when you are dealing with humans there is a need for "in your face agendas" throughout a calendar year to ensure that the customers' needs are front and centre of everyone's minds. Regular touchpoints and simple tools to take away allow your business to reinforce what 'good' looks like in a language that everyone can understand.

An important goal for Jason was to develop a customer-centric culture through empathy. He encouraged all dealership owners and managers to think more about the customer and put themselves in the customers' shoes:

> I think inherently everyone has it – empathy. But because of lived experiences we put up personas. And some people's way of surviving is not to show empathy because they feel (and it's right because it's their feeling), they feel that they're going to be seen as weak or that they are being challenged. I think everyone has the ability to be empathetic in a service environment. What organisations need to be able to do – and I'm not suggesting it's easy – is to make sure they put the right tools around their people,

so if they're not naturally comfortable being empathetic to a stranger they're still able to manage in that situation in a genuine way.

An example Jason referred to of when they started to focus more on seeing things through the customers' eyes was the time of day they assigned parents to come and collect their car:

> We get so focused on what's that one thing I can do that will take my score, my loyalty, my whatever, from A to B, that we forget that it's not actually one thing. It's one hundred little things every single day that make the difference. For example, when a mum with kids or a dad with kids needs to pick up their children from school at 3pm, then it is not helpful when you say their car's going to be ready at 3:30 in the afternoon. Have it ready at 2:30 because at 3 their kids need to be picked up and that will be their number one focus at that time.

This might sound like common sense, yet it is the single thing that Volkswagen have leveraged: more common sense.

Following on from the goal of developing more empathy in their culture, Jason discussed the need for reflection, particularly for leaders, as a fundamental practice. When we gather leaders together we talk at length about three things customers, I believe, measure us on:

1. First, did I have success and achieve what I wanted to achieve?
2. Second, how much effort did it take? Could I achieve the same success with less effort than I expected to?
3. Lastly, did I make a connection? Was the customer feeling valued, inspired or whatever the situation may have called for?

When you have success, effort and emotion working together, that's when you've delivered an experience that's memorable. When any one of those elements is missing, that's when people are merely satisfied (not wowed).

Reflection can be done in team meetings as Jason described, with a clear intent and purpose to learn from each other. It can also be as simple as asking staff these same questions at the end of the day, or end of month – review conversations where you encourage staff to make mental and physical notes of how effective their performance has been when it comes to empathy and understanding their customers.

Jason referred to two areas of the business performance that are contributing to a sustained uplift for VGA.

The first is that he believes the desired behaviours of leaders, when embedded, create a snowball effect of service throughout the network. He explained:

> One particular dealership owner missed the main conference this year and his mindset was fixed. He did not believe focusing on service was worth the effort or investment. After five days of observing one of his colleagues, who went to the conference and began implementing some of the behaviours, the owner realised that he needed to change also. He called me and said that he could now see that if he only looked at his business with a purely commercial lens and not a relationship lens then he was literally leaving money on the table. So I see one of the greatest impacts of relentless training and development is people learning from their own people.

The second is that turnover of staff is reducing. In the 18 months since they made a concerted effort to focus on the customers' needs, VGA has seen a reduction in the number of people who left to work elsewhere. The organisation still has a way to go in reaching the goal it has set on this particular metric, however what's important is where it has come from.

I learned that the staff turnover metric had not moved positively in 15 years until now and that has been seen in hard costs such as loss of productivity and the cost of recruitment. With these indicators improving, VGA is seeing a direct positive impact on the bottom line.

First people, then results.

MINDSET MOMENTS

1. Volkswagen Group Australia leads with empathy.
2. The company focuses intently on employee experiences, trusting that this will carry over into how employees support customer experiences.
3. Training and development is prioritised, unapologetically and relentlessly.
4. There are many 'in your face' moments throughout a year to ensure new employees are trained and existing employees are reminded about the empathy mindset.
5. VGA takes time to reflect on how it has succeeded in developing an emotional connection with the customer.
6. The company keeps it super simple with tools and conversations that represent plain common sense.

Customer metrics

- NPS (by Qualtrics).
- Employee Engagement (by Qualtrics).
- Team member retention.
- Customer retention.

Awards

- Customer Experience Management Asia Summit 2017: Bronze Award, Best Use of CEM Technology.
- Customer Experience Management Asia Summit 2017: Notable Mention, Best Customer Experience Team.
- LearnX 2016: Gold Award, Best E-Learning Design – Interactive Scenario (for online customer experience training).

Mindset 2: Questions

*If I had an hour to solve a problem and my life
depended on the solution, I would spend the first
55 minutes determining the proper questions to ask.*

ALBERT EINSTEIN

Remember the fable about the tortoise and the hare? The hare is intent on winning the race. It rushes around until it wears itself out. The tortoise, on the other hand, understands that slow and steady wins the race, that it takes bravery, humility and perseverance to get to where you want to go.

Leaders in organisations are mostly like the hare. We rush around from meeting to meeting, barely stopping to think about how we are interacting with ourselves, let alone our staff. We're multi-tasking, crossing off actions on our to-do list, so how on earth would we find the time to stop and reflect on our relationships with our employees or customers?

*As a leader, you are responsible for the people who are
responsible for your customer service outcomes.*

When we race around like the hare we miss opportunities to develop our staff so they learn and grow. We make the outcome the priority, instead of the process. Your role, your responsibility, is to develop and deepen the capability of your team members so they are motivated, willing and able to follow you towards your desired outcome.

You need to learn to ask questions of your employees about how they feel about work. You need to ask them questions so that they feel seen, heard and an important part of the process. You have to ask them questions instead of focusing on just the answers, on just the results.

You have to show a sincere interest in your employees as humans to help them grow into their role, and to help them facilitate the needs of your customers.

ASK, DON'T TELL

Remember what it was like when you were a kid and you were told to do your homework? I never truly bought into the idea of homework, nor did I willingly do the tasks. I (like many of you, no doubt) reluctantly forced myself to do it. It felt like a chore, a nagging item on my to-do list, a monkey on my back that weighed me down. I simply did not see the need to learn the topics nor understand why it was important when I was told to 'just do it'.

Any teacher, whether one for a classroom of fifth graders or in a workplace of 15 service staff, will be far more effective at turning around results when they ask instead of tell. No one likes being told what to do. Our employees are no different!

Telling our staff to deliver better service is not the way to create a healthy and successful service mindset.

In fact, when we tell people to focus more on better customer service we potentially create a counter-intuitive effect that will end up encouraging fake, insincere service interactions with customers.

A lot of the time we bark out orders and fixate on what we have to do to get the results. But we have to get to know our staff, to invest time in our employees, in order for them to deliver exceptional customer experiences. In busy service environments, leading with questions becomes a crucial skill. Your staff must be able to come up with innovative solutions on their own, especially when stretched outside of their comfort zone or under pressure.

When you ask questions, you encourage your staff to think for themselves, and ultimately to make better decisions that will benefit the whole organisation.

DEVELOP, DON'T DIRECT

Many of us say that one of the reasons we enjoy being a leader is because we feel deeply satisfied when we help develop our staff. It is satisfying to see people in our care grow. It is motivating when others around us are inspired by us, when they want to contribute to organisational goals and when they feel valued in their work.

The issue is that many of us, over time, become used to directing staff instead of developing them.

When you *direct* staff you:

- give them orders without reasons for doing tasks
- teach them to become dependent on you
- limit creative thinking
- encourage disengagement (and possibly enragement!).

When you *develop* staff you:

- ask them questions about how you might improve the process
- teach them to think for themselves
- enable greater creative thinking and problem solving
- encourage engagement.

Developing staff is a long-term game,
not a short-term solution.

If your relationship with your employees is always about directing them to do a task, their performance will plateau and their ability to perform in your absence will diminish. The reality of the service industry is that you are not always available to give the answers; you need staff to think on their own two feet and truly shine when you leave the room.

When you ask questions you actually start to lift your employees' performance because they feel part of your solution. They want to help you, they want to work with you! They are more likely to not only remember what to do, but also believe the importance of *why* they must do it.

This is what you are aiming for with each and every opportunity you have to connect with your staff, and it only comes when you ask (develop), instead of tell (direct) your employees what to do.

Imagine you are in a real-life work scenario, in which you walk past an employee and observe them behaving towards a customer in a way that is less than satisfactory. Within a split second you have an opportunity to decide whether you will:

- **tell** (direct) this employee what you observed and what you expect to see in the future when they interact with customers; or
- **ask** (develop) this employee to think about how they approached that interaction, what they brought to it, and what the impact of that was on the customer.

Our brain is so powerful that we also have the capacity, within that split second decision making, to make a choice to justify our decision, judge our decision and even predict the response of the employee based on our decision. The real work begins when wanting to lead with questions. The reason leaders resist the second option above is because it requires a level of presence, trust in the process itself and time to plan the questions; therefore the work-around or shortcut is to simply tell, instruct and direct.

If you want to enact real change in your team,
first they must see the need for change.

Look for clues

Being nice is only 20% of good customer service. The rest is about gleaning information to give the customer what they need. We are always on the hunt for clues.

We need to remind our employees that we ask questions to:

- obtain information
- help guide the conversation
- express our interest in the person
- clarify what a customer needs/wants
- explore a problem or a difficulty the person may be having
- encourage engagement in other products (not necessarily upselling).

What we are aiming for is to create rapport and connection with the customer – it may lead to an upsell but the questions need to be framed to make the customer feel like you are interested in them and not their money.

BE PRESENT, PROCESS, PLAN

To help build questions into your approach to leading a service culture, there are three areas you can work on.

1. Be present

As leaders, we need to ensure we spend a reasonable proportion of our time being physically present, and address issues as they occur, otherwise we will miss opportunities to coach our teams.

In the Unsung Hero story of Australian Unity (see page 88), we will see how side-by-side coaching was introduced for its contact centre employees, which highlighted for the organisation the importance of dealing with matters when they occurred and addressing mediocre performance at the time leaders witnessed it, not a month later in a scheduled team meeting.

Customer experience improved immediately from this development, thus saving many more customers from being negatively impacted. The new company process for developing staff required conscious leaders in the contact centre who were present to observe their teams and who were committed to dealing with what they observed in that present moment, daily.

Halt poor performance at an early stage and thoroughly check it before poor performance isn't self-corrected or becomes even worse.

2. Trust the process

Just like the tortoise in the fable mentioned at the beginning of this chapter, slow and steady is what wins the race. When we believe that we simply don't have time to address a situation through questions and that instead it is more time-effective to tell, we have the unhelpful mindset that faster is better and we are desperate for results rather than trusting a process of learning.

Faster is not always better and, in fact, seeing time as an obstacle is an example of staying fixed in a certain mindset which leads to your team also being stuck.

Remember that one pace does not fit all. We all learn at different paces and when you are leading many people, in some cases hundreds if not thousands of staff, you need to be mindful of this. There is no doubt that questions take time, mainly because we want our employees to process information and think about the topic raised. We must be patient and hold the space for our teams to process and learn.

Time is definitely a large hurdle for busy frontline leaders to get over. What if we were to look at time differently? We could spend more time upfront to properly address an issue to effect change, at the opportunity, instead of having to address the issue repeatedly over time because we simply repeat our ineffective response.

If I *tell* (direct) my five-year-old niece every time she comes to visit that she must put on her shoes when she goes walking in the garden, it would be a quick amount of time spent initially in that moment. However, I guarantee that every time she came to visit, I would need to repeat myself over and over again.

If I *ask* (develop) my five-year-old niece the first time she visits, what she would need to be mindful of when walking through the garden barefoot, we could then go into a conversation where she might offer up ideas such as being stung by bees, pricked by bindies or injured by nails left out by a workman. This conversation that got her thinking for herself, would make her realise the relationship between her safety and putting on her shoes.

Initially, the 'ask' conversation would take minutes more than simply telling her, however, I guarantee that the next time my niece came to visit she would not only wear her shoes in the garden but she would proudly tell me why she was wearing her shoes.

Trust the process: short-term pain for long-term gain. Rather than viewing time as an issue, consider how much time you might waste going over the same issue if you don't nip it in the bud now. Ask yourself:

How much time do I have now to help develop this employee in this moment? How happy am I to repeat myself over time?

3. Plan your questions

For years I used to think that if my team liked me then they would do as I say. Yeah, right! Over time I have learned that when we step into the role of serving our teams, helping them to be better than yesterday, then we actually do start to help them and they start to help us – whether they like us or not.

When we truly commit to something we give it great thought; we prepare for the task at hand. Committing to develop our teams requires preparing for the conversations we will have with them and knowing roughly the questions that we will ask.

Saying we will do something and doing it are two different things. We can all say we are committed to developing our staff, we can all say we are good leaders who like to help people learn and grow – but the reality is, the work of a leader necessarily involves upfront preparation time. The actual asking of the questions can also be hard, particularly when it is not your natural starting point as a leader.

We coach our staff in order to move them forward. This has a natural positive effect on our business. Thus we need to take some time in the planning of questions for coaching and developing staff in order to reap the best rewards. Remember our tortoise!

You must always prepare for a conversation with an employee, even if it's a two-minute one.

The questions that I most frequently encourage leaders to consider using when planning to talk to frontline employees specifically about their service performance are:

1. How do you think the customer felt in that interaction?
2. Where do you see some areas of improvement based on that last interaction?
3. What training do you think you may need to serve customers?
4. Why do I get the sense that you are a little distracted today and have some things on your mind?
5. In that interaction, when was there another opportunity to seek more information from the customer?

Of course, you never know where that conversation will go. All of these questions are based on the assumption that you have observed that the employee's behaviour towards service could be improved. The intention behind these questions is to start a conversation, with no expectation of where it may go.

This, again, may take time and you may find that this first conversation is the beginning of a few more. Trust the process. If you start here, you will get a better outcome in the long run, a more sustainable outcome for the employee and for the overall service towards customers.

A simple starting place in preparing for a conversation is:
What question will I ask?

Questions on the fly

Due to the nature of the service sector, it's not always possible to prepare for conversations thoroughly. We need to be able to ask questions on the fly as well.

If I am underprepared for any reason when entering a conversation with someone, or have been taken by surprise and want to develop the employee in the moment, I have three simple prompts to help me.

1. **Avoid closed questions.** Erase from your brain questions that start with: Do, Are, Can, Could, Will or Is. They will get you nowhere. All questions that start with these words lead to a dead end. "Can I help you?" is one of the worst questions you can ever ask someone in a service environment (employee or customer).

2. **Ask "Why?" five times.** The best default for developing people is keep asking why. You will go deeper into the conversation and it will buy you time to think more consciously about a specific question to help you get well on your way to co-creating a light bulb moment.

3. **Keep quiet.** This is grossly underutilised in conversations between leaders and employees. Often the silence is just enough to keep the employee digging deeper and talking more about what they believe is going on and the best solution. Try it and see.

RESIST RESCUING

The biggest challenge of learning to lead with questions is when we can see clearly what needs to be adjusted or tweaked and want to dive in to rescue, fix and correct that person. It is incredibly important to resist the need to have the answers and to tell them to your team. This is not serving them, this is not coming from a place of care – it's coming from a place of ego.

It is crucial that you hold the space for your team members to discover the answers themselves.

Being humble and letting ego take a back seat in conversations is easier said than done. It is so very human of you to want to show someone a better, faster, easier or more effective way. But remember your role as leader is to help your employees and team grow, to co-create solutions with you.

Great coaches in the world of sports show us how crucial a bit of tough love is when they want their people to grow and succeed. They expect hard work, dedication and commitment to the process, even the smallest elements of training, trusting they will bring the desired outcomes.

As Voltaire put it: "Judge a man by his questions rather than by his answers."

Reflecting on questions

1. How well are you asking questions of your employees currently? If you were to give yourself a rating from 1 (poor) to 10 (excellent), what would that be? Why and what could improve?
2. What do you notice when you ask staff questions?
3. How much are your staff dependent on you?
4. How often do you prepare for your meetings with staff by preparing questions?
5. What is one thing you could do more of, based on the approach of being present, trusting the process and planning your questions?

UNSUNG HERO: Australian Unity

"Ask even if you are afraid"

When you have survived 175 years in business, it would be fair to say that you are good at keeping up with the needs of your members and the broader community, and that you've somehow maintained your relevance and connection to your customers. This is Australian Unity in a nutshell. The kookaburra on the company logo is a strong national symbol for its customers to identify with, and the Australian consumer is always front and centre of Australian Unity's thinking.

Self-reflection is a key driver for this organisation, which is why I chose Australian Unity as my case study for the questions mindset.

James Heath, Customer Experience Manager, and Andrew Cass, Contact Centre Manager, at Australian Unity say the organisation is 'obsessed' with its customers. James explained:

> Historically we have always been customer obsessed;
> however, we are now looking at how we can bring this to
> front of mind for every employee, every day.

To cultivate the same customer-service obsession in its employees, self-reflection is key, James added:

> You look at the world, and the new technology coming out,
> and see consumer expectations are evolving and changing
> day by day. The same goes for employees. They too want to
> bring their whole self to work and be recognised as people,
> and so their expectations are forever evolving.

> For this reason, the status quo will never be good enough.
> When in business we must continue to innovate.

Self-reflection becomes a continuous thing that allows you to take actions that are far more effective and relevant to today's needs of the customer.

Two reflection activities that the organisation adopts with their employees are:

1. Roadshows at which leaders facilitate both the storytelling of learnings and celebrating customer service staff.
2. Workshops where all frontline leaders are asked to dissect what they do each day – not to try and 'catch them out', but to determine if there are tasks that can be removed from their day-to-day activities in order to free them up to do more side-by-side coaching with their team members.

Andrew explains:

We need to have human conversations with our people. Emails and digital communication is not enough. Ultimately if we are wanting our people to deliver great service, for me, it has to go both ways – it's not just about our members, service is definitely about our people. We work in a very dynamic environment and it's important that we keep our finger on the pulse. I find that employee surveys combined with face-to-face roadshows and workshops keep us close to our employees.

The approaches that Andrew talks about allow everyone in the organisation to stop and pause, even when things are busy, and evaluate the return on all of their efforts.

As a mentor once said to me, "Sometimes you are not in the best position to assess your own progress" – meaning that you cannot always see things objectively when you are deeply in something.

Organisations that build lasting relationships with their customers constantly ask their employees and customers, "How are we doing?" James went on to explain the benefits of leaders asking questions of employees and customers about what they value from the relationship, and clearly demonstrating that they are not afraid to ask.

> Looking at the last results from our People Poll survey, we can see that there has been an absolute shift in employee satisfaction [of those] who work in the contact centre. We ask the same Net Promoter Score question of an employee that we do a customer: "How likely are you to recommend Australian Unity as a great place to work?" We want to make sure that we are getting a balanced view of insights and we can then target some relevant initiatives to address some of the employees' concerns.

LISTEN TO GROW

Listen to Grow is a custom-built, enterprise-wide, feedback response ecosystem that supports a thriving business where people and customers feel valued and contributes to our goal to be a great place to work.

Without any meaningful data from your customers and your employees, it is very difficult to truly know the health of your business.

If you do not ask and be fully prepared to listen and take action in addressing what comes up, it's a pointless effort.

One of the examples that James and Andrew shared was a direct initiative from asking how happy the staff were and the response times of dealing with customers in peak periods, and the impact this was having on staff engagement in the contact centre.

Andrew explains:

> There are two times a year, which are peak times for insurance. On the first of April every health fund puts up their prices, on the same day. In March, members start calling us to discuss changes that are coming. We would go from 30,000 calls on average a month to 60,000 calls in March. This creates call queues, where members have to wait a little bit longer to be answered. We found from data that the engagement (happiness) of our customers and the engagement of our employees in the contact centre during that time both took a hit and decreased. We now have awareness as we move into March this year that this is a key focus for us in the contact centre. How we set up and actually manage our people is equally important to how we set up and manage our members. If we didn't ask we would never have had this insight to improve on.

Understanding what you are measuring and why you are measuring it is an ongoing process at Australian Unity. Asking for meaningful data is critical in order to stay in touch with employees and customers. However, you also have to be aware that sometimes metrics that are measured in a business are counterproductive and can negatively impact the mindset of employees and thus also impact customers.

An example of this was the average handling time of a customer call, that was measured in the call centre prior to

Andrew's arrival in the business. If you didn't make the average call time you were labelled as an underperformer, which was marked against your KPIs and impacted your overall performance, your remuneration and incentives.

Andrew explained how he saw this had a negative impact on their customers' experience, not just the employees' experience:

> When I first started to take over the centre, and I was listening to the calls and talking to my team, one of the things that came out as a red flag was that contact centre employees were too concerned about the time and the stopwatch, to meet the average call time, than actually servicing our customers.

> This led to calls being rushed, making mistakes, providing incorrect information and definitely dropping some of the humanistic side of our conversations, so we removed the metric immediately.

> We still do measure the call time, however, it is not an indicator of a KPI linked to performance. We are now more interested in: Did the customer's enquiry or issue get resolved? How well did the employee form a relationship with the customer?

In fact, when I walked into the call centre at the head office of Australian Unity for this interview, there was a buzz about the place. Leaders of the team were up and about, coaching and supporting their teammates, rarely sitting down at their desks.

As Andrew says:

> The leader's job, ultimately, is to be there to support our people, to coach and develop them through the best that they can do [in] each and every interaction. They are

definitely in real time supporting our people with enquiries that they may be struggling with, but also coaching and developing them on a regular basis to continually improve the service that we're delivering.

The way we regularly coach for development is by using information directly from our customers to help support our coaching plans, and look at ways we can actually improve, so it's very active, very colourful.

Prior to this, the coaching used to take place every four weeks in a meeting room, where statistics would be presented and then everyone would be expected to go out and improve. As a result, the lag time delayed the improvements implemented for customers and the development for employees was less impactful as it was not dealt with when the situation arose. Andrew says:

We have now moved our coaching out of a meeting room and introduced a real-time, side-by-side coaching framework, where the leader is actually sitting down with the employee, in real time, providing coaching and feedback when they are on the calls.

The additional benefit of this is that it is visually very powerful for everyone in the contact centre to see this, reinforcing that we are cultivating a culture that develops and supports people. For the employee who is being coached, it immediately empowers them and puts them in the driver's seat of their own development.

Additionally, Australian Unity provides real-time quality assurance measures from the voice of their customers on a dashboard that has been created for their leaders. This allows them to see a snapshot of real-time data, and gives individuals access to their own performance, seeing verbatim what customers are saying about them.

Side-by-side coaching from leaders coupled with access to their own dashboard has accelerated a culture of development and, as a result, a service mindset.

MINDSET MOMENTS

1. Australian Unity leads a service culture in which they ask questions.
2. Staff take an honest look at themselves through formal surveys and informal conversations.
3. Leaders are consciously aware of what they measure regarding customer service and know that what gets measured will guide what employees focus on.
4. Unnecessary steps have been removed for leaders to free them up, allowing them to spend more time with their teams, coaching them.
5. Transparency of what customers say about employees, through providing real-time data for employees to access at any time, accelerates employees' self-development and speeds up the improvements felt by customers.

Customer metrics

- NPS (by Qualtrics).
- Employee Net Promoter Score (eNPS) (by Qualtrics).
- Customer Satisfaction (CSAT) (by Qualtrics).
- Customer EFFORT (by Qualtrics).

- Complaints (measured inhouse).
- Retention (staff and members – measured inhouse).

Awards

Australian Unity has not been active in the CEX Customer Service Awards space over the last couple of years, as the company has been focused on getting foundational aspects right. Awards have, however, been achieved in the product space.

What its customers say

- "Very helpful and was able to articulate what the covers were that were best suited to me. Great service and also very quick to answer the phone."
- "Only just returned to AU after not being happy with another provider. Drew gave me better information about the cover and more confidence to come back."
- "Customer service was helpful in everyway [sic] possible way. The question [sic] were handled thoroughly. Highly recommended."
- "David was extremely helpful and was professional but also had a great manner. He was able to answer all my questions promptly and made our transition easy."

Mindset 3: Energy

You give life to what you give energy to.

Like the electrons that move from atom to atom to help create the charge or 'zing' of electricity that powers our appliances, we (employees) play a vital role in feeding energy into the quality of customer service to give it a 'zing'.

The energy mindset is about having an acute awareness of an employee's energy and how it transfers to the customer. Service, at its core, is a constant exchange of energy and energy is a large determining factor of the quality of service.

So what does a high-quality service interaction really involve? It first began to be defined in the late 1980s, when an academic by the name of Klaus presented a theory that explained that customer experiences are related to employee experiences. In other words, it was the first time a theory was presented that the happier the employee is during a service exchange, the happier the customer will be.

Chase and Stewart then evolved this theory into a definition of the three critical aspects that make up a high-quality service interaction:

1. Task (what must be done).
2. Tangible (physical surroundings and facilitating goods).
3. Treatment (the emotional and social content of the encounter).

Task is the desired output, process, procedure, scripts and decision-making activities that represent techniques and technology. For example, a task may be completing a transaction, with a distinct beginning and end.

Tangible means the servicescape, the elements of the interaction that are in the physical realm. They include things like the artefacts, temperature, lighting, sound, and overall ambience and feel of the environment based on the physical surroundings.

Treatment of the service interaction is primarily concerned with the relationship between the employee and customer. The social interaction is what becomes important here and it is what determines the customer's perception of their overall treatment.

Think of these three service ingredients like you're baking a cake – if any of them is miscalculated or neglected then you'll end up with a flat, tasteless cake.

Time and time again, I see businesses investing in the tasks and tangibles of their customer service touchpoints, but rarely do I see a business give an equal amount of energy to the treatment of the customer. This is the emotional connection piece, it's how someone (your frontline employee) makes someone else (your customer) feel. It's why the quality of customer service is often inconsistent and insufficient.

Think of emotional connection in this light:

- Just because our food is great and well-priced, doesn't mean we have permission to be arrogant when we serve it.
- Just because we have the best-looking bar on the high street, doesn't mean we have permission to ignore our customers' needs and keep them waiting.
- Just because we are renowned for delivering the fastest car service in town, doesn't mean we forget to build rapport and create relationships with our customers.

It is a very dangerous place to be if you believe that your tasks and tangibles are superior to any competitor and, therefore, how a customer is treated is less important. Sure, tasks and tangibles are important but it's how you treat your customers that keeps them coming back for more and feeling an emotional connection to your brand.

You need to give equal energy to the treatment of your customers, not just the tasks and tangibles that make up the whole service interaction.

FILL UP YOUR FUEL TANK

Consistent quality service interactions are the holy grail. They make life at work not only happier, but they are also the foundation from which customer loyalty can thrive.

So how might we describe a high-quality service interaction to our employees? Perhaps something like:

- smile
- be mindful and ask good questions
- listen to understand
- be informative and helpful
- anticipate what the needs of the customer might be
- follow process and procedures wherever possible
- find solutions
- be efficient and timely
- thank the customer.

How easy and perfect your service would be if every employee consistently delivered the above in some shape or form!

The reality, though, is quite different. In my observations and experience over an average shift length of eight hours, this is an unrealistic expectation of our frontline teams. Remember that we are dealing with humans, not robots, therefore what you are asking your employees to produce is endless energy that never runs out.

When it comes to managing our team, an essential element is managing our team's energy.

This means knowing where to put the aces and star performers in peak periods, knowing who to buddy up with whom when considering development opportunities, knowing when to schedule breaks and knowing when to roster people so they have a balanced lifestyle and some flexibility. These actions and decisions need to be made by you as the leader to manage the energy of your team and the impact that has on a consistent quality experience for your customers.

Just like a car needs fuel (energy), so do humans. We need to fill up our 'tanks' frequently and in order to keep track of how much energy is in our tank, we need to keep an eye on our fuel gauge.

When frontline leaders are performing at their best, they observe the energy of their teams and notice when they need to address the issue of a fuel tank that is almost empty.

SUSTAIN AND GAIN

A fantastic scenario that I witnessed years ago was in a busy department store during the Boxing Day sales. I noticed a manager walking the shop floor watching his staff. While I was busy jostling among crazy bargain hunters and shopaholics, I noticed him approach a member of his team and offer her some relief – to go out the back and grab some water and sit down for ten minutes – while he jumped behind the point of sale and took over from her.

This story leads me to believe that when it comes to sustaining energy for a customer, there are two types of approaches to service:

1. **Routine and lifeless approach to service:** An employee who is standing behind a point of sale register for several hours, doing a repetitive, tedious task in a mindless, transactional way. This mindset will create fatigue and exhaustion.

2. **Routine and full of life approach to service:** An employee who is standing behind a point of sale register for several hours, doing a repetitive, tedious task in a mindful, engaging way. This mindset will generate energy and connections.

When we make a choice to serve, we are making a choice to be a servant to others (our customers) and perform duties, at the direction or control of a company.

What images does that word 'servant' conjure up? Many of us think of someone who serves others in a home, domestically; a word that we wouldn't traditionally use in a workplace. However, let's consider the mindset of a servant in a private home and how that relates to customer service:

- **Real servants make themselves available to serve**
  They do what's needed, even when it doesn't seem convenient – ie, they don't have the right to pick and choose what to do or when to do it.

- **Real servants pay attention to needs**
  They do their best to properly understand what is needed and anticipate needs. Great opportunities to serve may be fleeting or appear when you don't expect them to. In order to make the most of these chances, when the time comes to serve another, your attention always needs to be out towards them.

- **Real servants do every task with equal dedication**
  The size of the task is irrelevant. The core criterion is: does it need to be done? Great opportunities often disguise themselves in small tasks. The little things in life determine big things.

- **Real servants do their best with what they have**
  Servants never say, "One of these days…" or, "When the time is right…" They just do what needs to be done. Less-than-perfect service that makes the most of the available resources is always better than service held back by wishful thinking.

We never refer to our staff as servants, but we do need to remember the heart of customer service is 'to serve'. What we are asking of our staff, minute by minute, hour by hour, is to be willing to give all their energy and whatever it takes to their customers for long stretches at a time.

It is through great service that we can sustain and renew our energy.

Maybe for some people in your business it does feel like they are a servant, in a negative way! That's why it's important that you learn to manage your team's energy correctly, because if they do feel like this then there is a reason why and you need to address it.

Many of us are generous at heart, and we are in the service industry because we want to be there. However, our energy gets consumed by our daily hectic schedules and life's demands. If you consider what might be going on for your employees, they may have a desire to give good service but for some reason (often due to fatigue or busy, distracted minds) they think they cannot afford to give it. "How can I give when I am barely coping myself?" is a recurring theme.

In fact, serving customers is the magic formula to generate even more energy. The energy you put out will always recirculate and find its way back to you.

The task of a conscious leader is to remind staff that it is through giving that we are happier and more energised. Service is not only a way of being, it is a whole way of life if we choose to view it as such. Shifting our energy, physically and emotionally, can be done by shifting our thoughts. As Buddha once said: "The mind is everything: what you think, you become."

The more we give, the more we receive.

A service mindset for life

Back in the early 1990s I worked at a fast-paced McDonald's. I was constantly bombarded with different competing instructions, taking orders from customers as well as fulfilling those orders.

One of the tools we had to trigger our service mindset was delineating between primary and secondary responsibilities.

If a customer came within two metres of us, we needed to acknowledge and address them immediately and everything about that customer became a primary responsibility. Secondary responsibilities meant everything else that did not directly touch the customer in that moment.

For example, a drive-through crew member's primary responsibility would be to take a customer's order, and their secondary responsibility would be to make up the cardboard drink holder trays when there were no customers to serve. The point being, when there is a customer in your presence they take first priority; everything else is a secondary priority.

This kind of service attitude is particularly critical in working environments that are full of constant distractions and demands, for example, a barista in a popular hole in the wall coffee shop who has to take orders, make quality coffee and ensure stock replenishment and that the coffee counter is presentable at all times. Or a sales assistant in a retail store has customers to welcome, customers who need assistance with a product question, customers who need to pay for a product and the general tidiness and presentation of the store to take care of.

This simple rule has stuck with me and created a service mindset for life. Try it and see.

HOW YOU TREAT ANYONE IS HOW YOU TREAT EVERYONE

Disney is renowned for its extraordinary service. Disneyland aims to create "the happiest place on earth". The philosophy is simple: it follows Shakespeare's famous words, "All the world's a stage, and all the men and women merely players." Disney teaches its teams to carry out their duties by performing like they are on stage, whether they are in front of customers or whether they are behind the scenes.

This is a way of life – the Disney expectation of attitudes and behaviours is that they are not something that you have and do only when you wear your uniform, they are a whole way of being (ie, whether on stage or off stage).

Whoever we are serving, wherever we are – whether customers or colleagues – our attitudes, tone of voice and behaviours all play a part in how we treat others. We all want to be treated the way we wish to be treated. This universal principle means you must treat your staff the way you wish them to treat your customers.

Your employees mirror your behaviours.

As simple as it may seem, reading it on this page, for some reason when employees put on their uniforms and go out on the shop floor to perform their duties, this principle is sometimes forgotten.

Take a moment to consider how you are treating your employees right now:

- What are some positive impulses you frequently exhibit with your teams, and how do they impact them?
- What are some negative impulses you frequently exhibit with your teams, and how do they impact them?
- How well do you know your teams?
- What's important to them?
- What words would an employee use to describe you to their friends or family members?
- How willing are your employees to do things for you? Do they respect you and will they follow you?

Now, how would your treatment of your employees rub off on them and impact how they treat the customers?

POSITIVE ENERGIES

In order for you to create an environment in which your people are fully engaged and happy you need most, if not all, of the following energies to be in play:

- Employees love what they are doing
- Employees look forward to coming to work
- Employees are passionate about what they do

- Employees feel that they are an important part of the big picture
- Employees understand customer needs.

DIRECTING ENERGIES

Being a conscious leader who is committed to cultivating a service mindset, to keep employees and customers happy, entails:

- Giving the team something to believe in
- Helping employees understand who they work for
- Helping employees understand their role in the light of a step change
- Showing them how to take ownership of what they do in their role
- Generating excitement about what the company could become/create and how it could positively impact the community.

As a leader, to increase your employees' engagement levels when interacting with customers, you must first tune into your employees' needs.

CULTIVATE THE GOOD

When it comes to improvement, we traditionally look for more ways to improve in areas where we fall down. We exert far too much energy looking at the gaps, weaknesses and poor performers in our business. Consequently, it can feel effortless and almost energetic when we focus our energies on looking for 'good'.

To cultivate a service mindset in your business
you need to look for and share the good service
interactions that already exist.

When you make the good stuff visible, when you give it the kudos, credit and attention it so rightly deserves, then it comes back to you in spades. Albert Einstein explained this best when he said:

> Everything is energy and that's all there is to it. Match the frequency of the reality you want and you cannot help but get that reality. It can be no other way. This is not philosophy, this is physics.

This carries over to your customers as well. When your employees give off the right energy, then your customers are more likely to respond to this in a desirable way. Aka: happy staff equals happy customers. Sharing your employees' 'good' stories will promote favourable behaviours in your organisation and help to improve the organisational culture.

When I visited one of my clients in the insurance industry, I was proudly invited up to his customer service team area on level four. Here, he pointed to a wall of green paper squares, each with a message on it. When I looked closer, each message was a compliment to a customer service agent from a customer.

My client told me that their goal as a team was to make the wall completely green. The messages weren't filed away in a folder, but visible for everyone (including visitors like me) to see. This was their way of sharing positive stories, of rewarding, recognising, learning and celebrating with each other and anyone who came into the office.

Sharing stories is as simple as asking employees at the end of each month for compliments they have received. You are looking for what characteristics they display when they are at their best and have made a customer happy. Unlike graphs and data, these stories will generate more excitement about the individual or team and help others imagine and realise what they are capable of accomplishing themselves.

Help your employees paint the wall green by giving conscious energy to your good news stories.

Reflecting on energy

1. How much energy is given to the treatment of your customer service interactions right now?

2. How have you articulated to your employees the way in which you wish them to treat your customers?

3. What energy are you currently bringing to your own interactions?

4. How do you 'paint the wall green'? What could you do better?

5. What are some ways you could improve in how you treat your employees, knowing this will impact their treatment of customers?

UNSUNG HERO: Melbourne Cricket Ground

"Give energy to customer service"

When you are the most iconic stadium in Australia, the beating heart of Melbourne, there are many eyes watching you and a weight of expectation. Established in 1853, the Melbourne Cricket Ground (MCG) has over three million visitors every year, from lifelong spectators, members and locals to national and international travellers. It is described on the MCG website as "more than just a sports venue. It's a place where memories are made and childhood dreams come alive." In short, it is full of energy, which is why it is my case study for the energy mindset.

When I walked into the venue to meet Donna Price, General Manager of People and Culture at the MCC, I could feel a certain energy in the place, like I was in the presence of greatness amid such a rich history.

At the time of my meeting with Donna, the MCG had just been awarded the Customer Service Project of the Year – Cultural Transformation Award – at the Australian Service Excellence Awards. I learned that this was the result of a three-year journey: and the journey began with deciding that customer service was a key strategic priority:

> This customer service project was born out of our strategic plan for 2016 to 2020, which has the customer at the centre of the plan.
>
> In a venue like the MCG there are many things to invest in. Over the years we have invested heavily in physical assets such as WiFi, scoreboards, upgrading facilities such as bars and dining outlets within the stadium itself, all of

which improve the overall customer experience. By making customer service a strategic priority, we were making a conscious decision to turn our attention to the quality of the human interactions of customer service and invest in the people of our business.

Highlighting that the customer is important is the first step in transforming a team's mindset to be less like a gatekeeper and more like a caretaker.

When something or someone is important enough to you, you look for ways where you can say 'yes' to trying new approaches and prioritise their needs. Following the first step of prioritising customers in its strategic plan, the second step for the MCG was to ensure that it had clearly defined what great customer service looks like, so anyone at any level can deliver on this expectation.

Donna explained:

> This is a very special place for people. For this reason, we not only have over one thousand event staff and a couple of hundred permanent staff, we also have three hundred and sixty volunteers who help us deliver an event or a tour experience. When it came to looking at our decision to become more customer-centric we had to consider various levels of skills across the workforce who come into contact with customers, and how best to educate those who have multiple touchpoints with the customer, so that's where CARE was born.

Establishing CARE (Courteous, Anticipate, Responsiveness, Efficiency) was the beginning of defining what great customer service needed to look like at the MCG and of addressing their greatest challenge in service: executing consistent customer service to one hundred thousand raving fans at once.

The challenge that any venue or stadium of this size has is achieving consistent customer service.

Consistency of service can only be addressed if everyone knows what is expected of them. As Donna explains:

> What really got in the way of us delivering exceptional and consistent customer service is that we really didn't have any clarity of understanding on what great service needed to look like. So we turned our attention to this and gave this energy.

With such a diverse mix of employees coming together to deliver an event, the MCG team made sure their customer service framework and key messages were simple and easy to remember, which gave clear focus to help build the program and embed it. By creating CARE it gave a framework including a shared understanding of what good customer service looks like through the lens of these four critical behaviours: being courteous, anticipating needs, being responsive and efficient.

Using behaviours in service, in real-life situations, increases the likelihood of the behaviours sticking compared to those presented in traditional service procedures. Procedures are tried and tested, proven and agreed on; however customer service is anything but routine and it is difficult to prescribe a procedure in such a dynamic environment as a stadium.

Employees who are interacting with customers do of course need a framework to take into account the context, what is going on around them and their service approach – which is influenced by the person they are serving. It's this that helps create a more relevant and personable interaction.

Donna shared with me how they have operationalised the behaviours in the venue and what practical tools assist with building momentum and energy behind customer service:

> Our biggest challenge going forward when we launched CARE was maintaining momentum beyond the initial hype and excitement. By recognising that customer service was a strategic imperative, this meant that we needed an actual program with initiatives including having a budget allocated to deliver these initiatives to reach many employees consistently throughout the year.
>
> - We implemented a CARE group including a good cross-section of people across the organisation, including contractors and partners, whose job it was to communicate and champion out in the venue.
> - We incorporated CARE into recruitment programs and selection criteria for hiring.
> - We replaced our previous A to Z guide with more area-specific information cards that gave employees information that was personalised and relevant to their area for an event, empowering them to assist the customer in the moment, with all the information they need at their fingertips.
>
> Our biggest learning in year one is that practical tools are crucial for large workforces who only come together once a week for six hours, so it's got to be easy and informative.

Practical tools that support behaviours in customer service are what helps large workforce teams to keep focused and concentrate their attention on what is important.

One of the great opportunities for customers who visit the MCG is the potential to experience something that creates, as Donna describes, 'goosebump moments'.

These can come from an artist performing on the main stage, an AFL player scoring the first points for their team or the one-minute silence on Anzac Day where 100,000 fans stand together in the stadium in silence to honour those who have served our country and lost their lives. These types of lifetime memorable moments are made every week in the MCG.

Furthermore, I was inspired to hear that by year two and well into year three of the customer service transformation program, there was a desire to create this similar energy of 'goosebump moments' when serving customers by delivering on the little things. Donna says:

> In year two, we piloted a CARE squad. The role of the CARE squad is to be roving customer service agents, dressed in blue, helping out at turnstiles, ticket booths and directional points of the stadium. Their remit was to create personal care and be fully accessible to any customer questions or needs during the event. A great example was a Brazil versus Argentina international football game: a family had bought the front row seats that night, very excited, until they got to their seats and realised there was a barrier in front of them which blocked their view of the field. The father had paid a premium for this experience with his family and was obviously disappointed. The CARE squad had the ability in the moment to recognise the issue and fix the problem by relocating him to a great vantage point.

With practical tools in place and a desire to draw out the passion in people who work at the MCG, by the time year three had come around, CARE was very much built around the stories at the MCG that employees felt had created 'goosebump moments' for them and their customers.

What I found extremely interesting when speaking with Donna was the decision to create a bespoke program that was unique to the MCG rather than pick up a best-practice model and layer it over its business:

> There was a decision at one point on the journey where we had to consider bringing in the Disney model to overlay into the MCG or tailor a program to reflect the MCC – who we are and what we do. I firmly believe now, three years in, that given the amount of pride and passion felt by most employees who worked at the MCG, we made the right decision to create CARE and tailor it to our needs. It is in fact the feeling of pride and passion from the employees that we now leverage. What things about the stadium give the staff 'goosebumps' and how will this make a greater impact on connecting the customer to these types of 'goosebump moments'?

Sharing 'goosebump moment' stories helps to deliver great service at the MCG.

MINDSET MOMENTS

1. The MCG leads a culture of customer service by giving energy to it and making it a key strategic priority.
2. The organisation works with the passion that exists with employees and gives them practical tools to apply in their roles.

3. It has built-in energy and momentum to drive its service mindset by focusing on four critical behaviours (being courteous, anticipating needs, being responsive and efficient) – and keeping it simple.
4. Tailoring a customer service program may seem like far greater work initially but the resulting employee behaviours and attitudes will have a greater chance of being ingrained into the culture operationally.

Customer metrics

Customer service as part of Match Day satisfaction for both AFL and Cricket seasons includes:

- The arrival and departure experiences
- The food and beverage customer service
- Service satisfaction for the general public/casual ticket purchasers and members on event day
- Every six months, the overall member's experience
- Every two years, employee alignment and engagement.

Awards

- 2017: Winner, Melbourne Cricket Club (stadium manager at the MCG), Customer Service Project of the Year – Cultural Transformation Award, Australian Service Excellence Awards.
- 2017: Winner, Melbourne Cricket Club – Best Achievement in Venue Management, Australian Event Awards.
- 2016: Melbourne Cricket Club, Service Champion, and Finalist for Customer Service Project of the Year, Australian Service Excellence Awards.

Mindset 4: Heart

When we bring heart to a conversation we meet people where they are at.

It was a mid-week evening. I was tired and a little distracted. It's fair to say that I didn't want to be shopping at the supermarket at 8pm. I was there in body, going through the motions, getting some veg for dinner.

Hannah, a teenage girl, served me. She immediately picked up on my energy levels and lack of engagement. She observed, "You just want to get home, don't you?" "Is it that obvious?" I replied. Hannah said, "I can just tell. At least it's quiet tonight and not too busy. I'll go as fast as I can to get you out of here."

She didn't do the standard, "How's your day been?" Instead, Hannah read my facial expressions and body language and could tell from my silence that I was not up for any small talk. She used her judgement to relate to me on a personal level, showing me that she understood what I was feeling.

Then she went that one step further, and matched her service speed to suit my needs. She started processing my items like she was training for the scanning Olympics. She used common sense and treated me like a human being with needs, instead of like a number. I felt seen, heard and understood.

This simple act of service is an example of how you serve wholeheartedly. Hannah served me from the best possible place she could in that moment. She didn't use fancy words and there was no fake smile or forced greeting like she was being compliant. As a result, the experience was authentic and meaningful and I felt like a friend, not a stranger on the other side of the counter.

If I compare my feelings after the experience to how I felt before I was served by Hannah, she certainly moved me in a positive direction and lifted my spirits in that moment. That supermarket, consequently, ranked higher in my mind as a place I would return to, just because Hannah treated me like a person and understood my deeper needs, not just my superficial need to buy food. Remember, the heart of service is human.

The heart of service is human.
This is the essence of customer connection.

From transactional to transformational

The supermarket scenario I recounted above could have gone in a completely different direction had Hannah said the following:

- "Hi, how are you?'" (even though I was visibly tired); and
- "Have a nice day," (even though it was 8pm).

In fact, I was expecting (and dreading) this type of typical transactional greeting and parting. It's likely I would have responded in much the same fake way:

- "I'm good, thanks," (because I really just wanted to get home) and
- "You have a nice day too," (because I couldn't be bothered engaging).

This is the same kind of empty and transactional experience we can get from a robot or self-serve kiosk.

When we transact with our customers in that way, we are wasting an opportunity to interact human to human, to turn a negative interaction into a positive one that could make or break the reason your customer returns or not.

As Dale Carnegie, author of *How to Win Friends and Influence People*, said: "When dealing with people, remember you are not dealing with logic, but creatures of emotion."

NOTHING SERVED, NOTHING GAINED

Imagine if we all worked for nothing – no money, no employee benefits, no car allowance, no travel perks. Instead, we volunteered our time and efforts; we 'served' in the truest sense.

A willingness to serve means giving all you have and expecting nothing in return. As a human, you naturally do this. You might have:

- noticed a stranger on a bus who needed a seat and you stood up and offered yours to them
- listened to a student or an employee who asked for your help and you gave them some advice
- made yourself available for a friend or neighbour moving house on their own

- stayed back late at work to help a struggling colleague, knowing you wouldn't get paid for the extra hours.

This is what it is to 'be in service'. It is knowing that your act or deed will make someone's day better, will impact them in a positive way and make both them and you happier.

It may seem like a small, inconsequential act, but you are delivering with willingness, wanting to be there, helping that person out and expecting nothing in return.

As we explored in the previous chapter, being willing to serve with a boundless amount of energy requires a 'giving' mindset – even in those times when you think you have nothing left in the tank. When we bring heart to a service interaction, we are tapping into the ultimate desire of any human: happiness.

We humans make the simplest things so complicated. Serving with heart is an act of love. We all have the ability to love. It is supremely simple, requires no training whatsoever, and the more you give love the more it increases.

Nothing stands between us and love, other than our egos which are rooted in our minds. Service requires leaders to prioritise heart over mind.

When we serve with heart, we are happier.

LEAD WITH HEART, NOT HEAD

The problem right now is that our workplaces, organisations, retail outlets and front-facing shops are undergoing some kind of identity crisis.

Our service staff deliver less than average service interactions because they have somehow forgotten that the heart of service means being a good human. Instead, our identities are all tied up in the job or a particular role. People treat what they do every day as just something they do every day. There is no heart in what they do. It's just a job they are being paid to do. They've forgotten they are there to serve – but it's not their fault. They are not 'bad' or 'wrong'. They have just forgotten.

The world is being strangled by the absence of love. It seems so obvious to me that service has the ability to transform this absence to abundance. Is that not a good enough reason to want to create a service mindset among your teams? It could not only transform the way you approach your work and your relationships, but could help humanity in a multitude of ways.

As leaders, it is our responsibility to ensure our teams are leading with heart and that they never forget that their primary purpose is to make customers happy.

How easy does that seem? Yet most businesses have made service difficult. We have introduced complex strategies, processes and procedures; we have made it a function instead of a feeling.

I see many businesses that are aspiring to create a customer service mindset and culture suddenly drop service standards into the business, alongside menial tasks like instructions for operating equipment, rules around risk, compliance and other protocols. This is not the way to develop customer service, because steps of service no longer resonate for service staff. They are instructions from the mind rather than intentions from the heart.

It is up to us to inspire confidence in our frontline staff, to give them reasons to love what they do, to encourage them to approach their role as a service and treat every one of their (your) customers as a human who wants to be happy.

Drop the six steps of service

Back in the 1980s, the service training at McDonald's was extremely regimented and systematic. One of the standard procedures for anyone working front of house (at the service counter) was to learn, memorise and master the six steps of service (greet, order, collect, prepare, deliver, thank).

Nowadays, these steps of service are delivered by automatic, digital self-serve kiosks and touch-pad screens with the same six steps embedded into the sequence that a human once delivered.

Steps of service used to be what we defined as best practice. However, what worked back then no longer works now, and that is why it has been automated.

Prolific author and marketing expert, Seth Godin, in his book *Tribes* explains that we are now living in a connection economy, which means we have to leave the industrial economy mindset behind and look for personal, relevant and meaningful connections to a brand and its people.

The industrial economy realised cheap, obedient labour was needed – people would sit still and do what they were told – but today's economy is very different and requires a different approach. The world has moved on, and so you need to as well.

The steps of service limit connections between employees and customers. We can get routine, repetitive, transactional, systematic, consistent service from a kiosk, a machine or a robot. What we ask of humans who are serving humans is that they connect, make it a personal interaction, make it unique, make it meaningful.

A MEANINGFUL MINDSET

Employees with a 'this is just a job' mindset create copy-and-paste customer interactions, meaning that they treat each and every customer as exactly the same (which, as individuals, we are not).

These employees use tone of voice, body language and conversation that are irrelevant to the situation. Quite often they will say things that seem out of context: for example, "Have a nice day" when it's really late at night or the customer clearly is not having a good day. They also fail to recognise repeat customers. How annoying is it when the shop assistant fails to notice that they just served you the day before – or worse, hours before?!

They miss valuable opportunities to not just make someone's day, but also make the organisation's brand memorable, for the right reasons.

On the other hand, a willing employee with a meaningful mindset – which overlaps in many ways with the heart mindset – is someone who loves being in service. They bring high relevance and meaning to each and every customer interaction.

They recognise when you're having a bad day (like Hannah did at the start of this chapter). They recognise you when you come into the store a second or third time. They say, "Great to see you again, what's your name?"

When your team members are willing, ready and able to serve, it automatically increases their discretionary effort. In turn, this increases the results for your business.

You want to encourage employees to go above and beyond their duties, seize any opportunity to serve and effortlessly strive to make someone's day.

Don't miss the moments to recognise and reinforce positive service behaviours when you see them.

Staff with heart

One of my clients has developed a service program called 'Heartbeat' and its monthly newsletter is called *The Pulse*. This is its main communication platform for sharing all the good news stories around the organisation. It is a brilliant way to reinforce what 'good' looks like in service.

Below is a direct extract from *The Pulse*. You will notice that in the crafting of this story, their values of service are in bold text to highlight to others how these values look when seen in action – very clever.

Vanessa had to display her service values when dealing with one particular customer. On a particularly quiet afternoon, with only one of the two registers operating at the time, a customer approached the counter and stood directly in front of the «REGISTER CLOSED» sign, placed her item (an ice cream) on the counter, and simply pointed at it as an indication that she was ready to purchase.

When Vanessa explained that the particular register was closed, but she would be able to assist at Register 2, the customer took the opportunity to swear and throw her ice cream towards Vanessa. At this point, she had to choose between responding in kind, refusing to serve the customer, or to 'kill her with kindness'.

*To her credit, Vanessa decided to show the utmost customer service to someone clearly having a bad day, completing the purchase with an extra-kind and understanding attitude. She showed **Respect** for a customer without knowing what she may personally have been going through, took **Ownership** and showed absolute **Courage** in a difficult and potentially unsettling experience, remained **Positive**, and did her best to **Simplify** the experience to enable the transaction to be completed as quickly as possible for the customer.*

A safe and secure workplace for all team members is non-negotiable for us in our organisation but Vanessa showed that a little heart, especially in what can often be a stressful airport environment for a customer, can go a long way.

The power of reinforcing behaviours when we see service staff serve with heart has a huge impact on a team's motivation, sense of pride and overall engagement with the company.

TRUST IN YOU

How a customer feels about an interaction with your employee is how that customer feels about your brand itself. It only takes one frontline person to have a less than average experience or a negative impact on one of your customers to risk you losing that customer for good.

If a telco provider says it will have an employee at your place by 4pm and they don't show up, you as the customer would probably say, "That company sucks." If a flight attendant is a little abrasive or doesn't attend to your needs on a flight, the customer may well say, "That airline sucks."

Your business might be doing one hundred things right, but it only takes one thing to completely destroy the trust you've built.

Customer contagion is a term inspired by the phrase "emotional contagion" coined by American psychoanalyst Gerald Schoenewolf. We can extrapolate from his definition of emotional contagion as shown in the bracketed text: "a process in which a person [employee] or group [business] influences the emotions or behavior [purchasing behaviour] of another person [the customer] or group through the conscious or unconscious induction of emotional states and behavioral attitudes."

In a world where we have become desensitised, it can be easy for businesses and employees to ignore how important emotion is in engendering a sense of trust, loyalty and commitment to a product or service. How you tap into your customers' emotions is how you impact the connection you have with them at the time of purchase and every interaction from that point on.

Think of it like a mirror. Your customer will feel the way your employee feels. During an exchange between an employee and customer, if the employee doesn't love or believe in what he or she is serving or selling, the customer will sense it. Trust will begin to break. In fact, when researching for this book I discovered scientific evidence that explains emotional contagion further. The electromagnetic field created by the human heart is actually 5,000 times more powerful than the electromagnetic field created by the mind. This evidence actually proves that people can feel that electromagnetic field five to ten feet away. This is just something you can't fake.

Your heart really does speak louder than your words.

How healthy is your heart?

When you are loving what you do, it will have a huge impact on how your employees love their service.

If we want to be of any use to others, first we must be brave enough to look in the mirror and see who we've become as a leader. Here are some reflection questions to ask yourself. There's no judgement, no right or wrong – just do a quick health check on how much you love what you are doing:

- What do you love about service? Why?
- What do you love doing at work? Why?
- Who do you love doing it for? Why?
- What do you gain by loving being in service?
- Where else might you get this in your life if it wasn't at work in a service environment?

APPRECIATE EVERY MOMENT

Above all else, remember that heart starts with you. Cultivating a service mindset in your organisation requires *you* to love being in service, not just your staff.

To achieve this, think about what you appreciate every day. Appreciation talks directly to our hearts and is a sure way to build relationships and connections with customers and your employees.

Remind yourself to be grateful, regardless of what you're working on or who is paying for the service or product. Reflect on the following when considering how best to grasp appreciation and bring heart to every people interaction:

- My work gives me opportunities to learn from others.
- Meeting customers is an opportunity to create further connections.
- Without my customers, there is no work or opportunity for me in this job.
- When I leave here (work) today, I will be a customer seeking what they seek.

When you truly start to appreciate every day for what it is – an opportunity to serve – then you bring heart into your work and your life.

Reflecting on heart

1. Think about a time when a staff member performed with the customer's best interests at heart while under extreme pressure. How did you recognise and reward that employee? If you didn't, what could you do next time?

2. What data have you got in your business that gives you a sense of how happy your customers are?

3. What activities or opportunities – for example, a volunteering program – do you have in your workplace to reinforce what it feels like to be in service and give without expecting anything in return?

4. When did you last recognise someone for going above and beyond in service, just doing something small to make someone's day?

5. How healthy is your own heart? (See the health check questions on page 126.)

UNSUNG HERO: Hudsons Coffee

"Serve from your heart"

Hudsons Coffee, owned by Emirates Leisure Retail Australia (ELRA) is a company Australians know and many love. Australia (no less, the world) has become a nation of coffee snobs and Instagram food critics. Food and beverage businesses at the best of times are fighting for any margin they can get. It's a tough industry, particularly in coffee.

There are now more specialty coffee shops popping up than ever before and the coffee chains make up only 5% of the Australian coffee market.

Food and coffee are emotional purchases for customers, and the businesses that are thriving, not just surviving, recognise this and connect to their customers by winning over their hearts rather than their minds. Hudsons is one such company, hence they are profiled here to showcase mindset 4, heart.

Managing Director of ELRA, Adam Summerville, highlighted the main challenge that Hudsons Coffee faces in today's competitive marketplace:

> As a brand in a competitive food and coffee market, our greatest challenge is consistency. We have to make sure we have a promise that customers expect and that it's consistency no matter what store they visit. We have a store in Darwin, Perth, Burnie (Tasmania). Getting consistency through your product and your people is hard.

Adam understands that you can never stand still and you always have to look at ways to improve – and that your key differentiator to the competitor is your service.

We can get great coffee and food from many places, but it's whether you strike up an emotional connection with your customer that determines whether they will come back for more.

Hudsons Coffee is a familiar brand, with an unchanged coffee blend for the past 20 years. ELRA is preparing to open the one hundredth Hudsons Coffee store in Australia later in 2018. Adam says:

> Knowing your product and knowing how to guide a customer with products is a critical skill in the food and beverage retail business. Leveraging the value of products through telling the story of where the product came from, the origin, connects the customer to the whole experience in that moment.

Adam and I agreed that the greatest threat to any brand is the humans involved in the process. How to achieve consistency from employees each and every day is Hudsons Coffee's greatest challenge, which is why the company includes product stories, sharing the story of the brand with staff in training sessions and connecting the heart of the business and the products with the people who are selling them. Adam shares an example:

> An employee comfortably talks through the choice of coffee blends with a customer. From here they can take this one step further and even inform the customer of the origin of the bean. This is really delivering on a connection to a brand. We have a Net Promoter Score (NPS) program in our business and we see an uplift of 30% in customer

satisfaction around their coffee when they are asked if they would like a choice of blends.

This is an example of serving with heart – being prepared to serve someone in a way that lifts their spirits and makes their day. When an employee has a narrative like this they are able to inspire customers and build greater rapport with them.

Employees are taught to ask customers how they are feeling, with the aim of guiding their product selection, creating trust and giving customers confidence that they are in good hands.

In fact, the company actively recruits people who are passionate about food and beverages. Adam explains they made a conscious decision to only seek a certain type of employee, knowing that if they want to be in this industry they will be a better fit than someone who is simply looking for a job:

> There's one of our staff, Adele in one of our bars in Brisbane airport. I love going there. Adele is so passionate, she is so detailed, a real service hero in my eyes. Half the time I go, Adele never knows I am there, but I can hear her talking to customers and it's unbelievable. She knows her product, she learns so much about the customers by asking great questions, she remembers their name during the service period and never seems to be stressed or distracted.
>
> I wish we could clone Adele. The reality is, that not every employee is like Adele and if it was that easy then we wouldn't be required in business. So it is absolutely up to the leaders on the floor to identify what good looks like and inspire others to do more of that. Be more like Adele.

Adam admits that he checks TripAdvisor and his NPSs multiple times a day. This is his way of seeing how much heart is being delivered across the network. Having this visibility is his way of getting a sense of how well each and every store, from the bottom of the country in Burnie to the top of the country in Darwin, are delivering quality service consistently.

I learned that after embedding an NPS program into the business for two years now, they were able to clearly tell a narrative to the Hudsons network. The figures show that the stores which have the higher NPSs also have the highest performing sales. This direct correlation is constantly referred to in team meetings and conferences to highlight that happy customers equals happy profits.

Hudsons specifically found that:

- The stores in the top third of the NPSs (ie, more than 70% overall satisfaction) are experiencing an average 3% positive transaction growth in their sales.
- The stores in the bottom third of the NPSs (ie, less than 50% overall satisfaction) are declining -4% in transaction growth.

Essentially, there is a 7% difference in real terms, based on NPSs.

One of Hudsons Coffee's core values is quality and a key behaviour for this is to never compromise quality. These customer survey measures are a great real-time indicator of how well the company is living up to what it promises.

The business, like most food and beverage operations, is a morning-to-night operation, spread across many different high-traffic locations such as airports, hospitals and high-street shopping centres. So there is a need for employees to adapt their service depending on the customer in front of them, depending on the time of day, peak periods versus slow periods, diverse cultures and languages. These are all real factors that a barista or team member must work with, every minute of every shift.

For this reason, leaders need to be able to inspire employees – connecting with their hearts rather than their heads – if they want their frontline teams to adapt their style of service and make an emotional connection with the customer. Adam refers to this as 'changing gears':

> Leaders both supporting the operations and leaders on the floor working with the frontline need to be able to change gears with their teams. If you are always in first gear and you are revving too high all the time, your wheels are going to spin. And if you are in fifth gear all the time you are going to run over the top of people, so we must know how to shift up and down gears depending on the people we are leading and the customer we are serving. The better we can adapt determines the better we can inspire.

> It is the operational leader on the floor who is responsible to kick-start, ignite a spark or change the gears of the team when the different day-part trading of a shift takes place. The way teams serve coffee in a busy airport coffee store at 5.50am is very different to how they serve coffee at 10am in that same store.

Adam's passion for leaders to be great role models in service really came through in our conversation. What I love about this is that when we are aiming to inspire staff and we ask them to bring their whole selves to a service interaction, we have to be able to show people how. It is not good enough to ask staff to be kind and to care in service interactions. We need leaders to show staff how – and this makes Adam a great role model to all his team. Adam consistently walks his talk:

> I love walking into a bar or coffee store when they are busy and under the pump, roll my sleeves up and help out. The other day I got off a plane at Melbourne Airport, saw our store was under the pump so I straightened some sandwiches up for them. Now I have no idea if any of the staff recognised me or thought I was a mad man, but that's not the point. There were ten people in a queue, they were under the pump and I needed to jump in and help out.

> I expect all support office staff or any senior leaders to do the same. In fact, we have a rule in our business that if you are travelling for work, you must arrive one hour earlier than you need to for travel and go and visit the stores, have an experience, help out if you can and be seen by the teams and interact with them. This is what earns respect and this is what gets you closer to the business and ultimately your customers.

Leaders don't force their teams to follow, they invite people to join their journey.

The insights I took away from my time with Adam and the team at Hudsons Coffee is that a great brand can be built, but it's the people who connect with the heart of the brand that keep it alive.

Giving staff stories and narratives to help them understand what is behind your brand and products are simple methodologies that keep the heart of your business pumping.

MINDSET MOMENTS

1. Hudsons Coffee has not only inspired people's senses but it has attracted leaders who see their role as inspiring people.
2. It keeps its leaders close to the operations by insisting that they roll up their sleeves and show their team members how it's done.
3. Hudsons is obsessed about delivering a brand promise and never compromises on quality.
4. It seeks passionate food and beverage employees who want to serve customers and who want to be inspired.
5. It tracks, monitors and rewards service against NPSs and continually highlights the correlation of scores to better performing stores in sales.

Customer metrics

-   NPS.
-   Customer loyalty.
-   Employee engagement scores.

Awards

-   FAB 2017: Airport Coffee or Non-Alcoholic Beverage Shop of the Year, Regional Winner (ASPAC) – Airport Coffee or Non-Alcoholic Beverage Shop of the Year – Emirates Leisure Retail; Hudsons Coffee, Sydney International Airport.
-   FAB 2016: Best Airport Coffee Shop – Emirates Leisure Retail; Hudsons Coffee, Brisbane Airport.

Mindset 5:
Purpose

*Efforts and courage are not enough
without purpose and direction.*

JOHN F. KENNEDY

The first question I ask a client right at the beginning of their customer-centric journey with me is:

*What is the purpose of your organisation
beyond making money?*

The Simon Sinek movement 'Start with Why' explains that people don't buy *what* you do, they buy *why* you do it.

Whether it be skincare, food, cars, toys, books or services, we are all able to provide a reason why we are interested in a brand or support certain products. Customers look for commonalities in your business, searching to see if you have similar values and similar beliefs.

As Benjamin Hale in *The Evolution of Bruno Littlemore* puts it:

> ...we, and I mean humans, are meaning makers. We do not discover the meanings of mysterious things, we invent them. We make meanings because meaninglessness terrifies us above all things. More than snakes, even. More than falling, or the dark.
>
> We trick ourselves into seeing meanings in things, when in fact all we are doing is grafting our meanings onto the universe to comfort ourselves. We gild the chaos of the universe with our symbols. To admit that something is meaningless is just like falling backward into darkness.

As humans, and as customers, we have a need to surround ourselves with people who believe what we believe. When we are surrounded by people who believe what we believe, trust emerges, which is critical for any kind of long-term relationship, even – no, especially – in sales.

Becoming clear about the purpose of your organisation is another way of becoming clear on what you believe in and what you value as a whole team, and this is a critical step in building trust with customers.

Clarity of your purpose is crucial to motivating employees, who are crucial to attracting your customers.

ARTICULATE THE WHY

Content does not make sense without context. Imagine that you gave instructions to someone to complete a large jigsaw puzzle. You gave them all the pieces (content) of the puzzle but withheld the top of the box that had the complete picture of the jigsaw (context). In other words, you instructed them to do a task that has no obvious meaning or purpose.

The person doing the jigsaw puzzle would be confused and it would take them longer to find momentum and connect to what the whole picture of success looks like. Possibly the activity would be short-lived, due to them becoming disengaged and quitting. It takes a deal of patience to complete a jigsaw without seeing the whole picture first.

Employees would much rather connect with *why* they are doing a task than simply what the task is. They would rather know how their small role is contributing to something far greater than themselves individually than just rocking up to a job and taking a wage each week.

When employees feel that they are surrounded with people who believe what they believe in, then they are more confident to stretch themselves and take risks when performing at work.

Equally, because they are in an environment of trust where they feel supported, they know that someone is watching their back and therefore they will be happier in this place; they will feel they belong.

So your purpose as an organisation is the greatest context you can provide to any one of your employees. Many of us will spend a large percentage of our life at work, and it's important that we work in a manner and a place that allows work to be a meaningful experience.

Today, people want their work to give them the opportunity to explore and experience what it means to be a human being. Our job as leaders is to help that desire to be achieved.

Once we can articulate our organisation's purpose, this then creates a values-based culture, along with positive interactions with employees, which builds trust and engagement.

Trust and engagement results in employees who are driven to interact with customers positively, which leads to customers who trust and recommend you to others.

IT'S MORE THAN SELLING FRIDGE MAGNETS

A company with a retail business in airports came to me with a query about how to get their staff excited about selling fridge magnets. The owner of the business spoke to me at length about his story and what got him into the business in the first place. At the end of the conversation he said, "If I could sum up what I am hoping for every day, other than selling loads of fridge magnets and earning money, it would be that I would want to make sure that everything we do leaves a positive and memorable feeling."

This is what we mean by purpose and a purpose statement. What he explained was *why* he got up each day and did what he did. With that one line, "everything we do leaves a positive and memorable feeling", the owner had a purpose much bigger than he ever imagined he could articulate to existing and new employees.

Purpose really is as simple as that – acknowledging what the spark is, why you set out to do what you do.

A great purpose must be:

- outwardly focused
- aspirational and belief driven
- long term
- humanistic
- broader than the company activities, products or services
- aligned to the company's values
- attractive to customers, employees and partners.

Your role as a leader is to help your frontline staff see they are an important part of your organisation's whole success story. So you need to explain what the whole picture of success looks like – you need to explain your purpose.

Richard Branson, for example, has built an enormous empire that is the Virgin brand based on the group's purpose: 'Changing business for good.'

As stated on the Virgin website, changing business for good means:

1. Thinking about the long-term impact of the business decisions that we make today.
2. Having a clearly articulated, embedded and measurable purpose in every Virgin business that drives their decisions and fuels their success, resulting in positive impacts on customers, people, communities and the environment.
3. Embedding our purpose, principles and values in all existing and new business investments.

4. Pioneering systemic change beyond the Virgin Group through Sir Richard Branson's profile and advocacy as a global business leader and rising to the challenges.

Now compare the Virgin brand example to a hypothetical small coffee shop down the road. It may have a purpose that is simply to "leave people better than you found them".

The coffee shop then describes what leaving people better than you found them means:

1. Always make sure people leave smiling or laughing.
2. Greet everyone by name if they have been here before.
3. Make sure the coffee is nothing less than perfect, just the way the customers like it.

Regardless of how small or large a business is, no matter how superficial or important the business solutions may seem: everyone can have a purpose beyond making money.

PRIORITISE PURPOSE AND PROFITS WILL FOLLOW

In *Culture of Purpose*, Deloitte's 2014 core beliefs and culture survey, a strong sense of purpose is defined as "a focus on making a positive impact on customers, employees and... society in general".

Punit Renjen, the Chairman of the Board of Deloitte LLP, explains:

> The data highlights the connection between a sense of purpose and the confidence required to sustain a successful business. The findings reinforce also the need for leaders

to not only articulate that purpose but to visibly and consistently live by those standards every day.

Purpose messages are often designed for an internal audience – your employees – but they can also be displayed publicly. I encourage my clients and teams to incorporate their purpose in all collaterals for internal training and communication purposes. I also encourage that same message to be shared on their website and social media channels.

Some famous purpose statements that were designed simply for internal purposes but have captured people's attention far more widely are:

- The Ritz Carlton: We are Ladies and Gentlemen serving Ladies and Gentlemen
- Zappos: Delivering Happiness
- Google: To organize the world's information and make it universally accessible and useful
- Walmart: We save people money so they can live better.

In the Unsung Hero section at the end of this chapter (see page 149), we see that the purpose of Bendigo Bank is to be 'Australia's most customer connected bank'. From my time spent with the team at their offices, I learned that this purpose was their true north in all decisions that were made at the frontline right up to the senior leadership team.

I saw this in all the collaterals, training materials and back-of-house areas. Even in the discussions we had around the bank's metrics and measurements, it was apparent that this purpose was translated into decisions and practices such as:

- Choosing to have local Australian staff employed in the contact centre and not offshore staff – the bank wants its customers to feel connected by employing people like its customers.

- Doing deep analysis on who its customers are, listening to them and recognising their wants and needs – the bank wants its customers to feel connected by actioning things that matter to them.
- Being active in the community with events, fundraising and helping individuals in a multitude of ways outside of banking – the bank wants its customers to feel understood and closer to people who work at the bank, like they are friends who care, not nameless bank tellers.

When customers and competitors see these types of actions and messages, they cannot help but sense that there is more depth to your organisation than making money. They start to really believe in what you believe in.

When belief in your organisation grows, this is when you actually start to make more money and when you start to have an impact on your bottom line – because this is where customer loyalty grows from.

VALUE WHAT YOU DO

Having a purpose that connects everyone to something bigger than themselves, and a set of core values to live by, is the glue for cultivating a service mindset in your teams.

A set of core service values will not only help remind your staff how to achieve your purpose, it is also one of the most effective tools for organisations to use to articulate and maintain a desired service culture. Service values can help define best practice. You can show through values in action what a good quality service experience looks like.

In his book, *Taking People with You*, David Novak quotes Howard Schultz, the CEO of Starbucks, on why organisations need values:

> The only thing we have is one another. The only competitive advantage we have is the culture and values of the company. Anyone can open up a coffee store. We have no technology, we have no patent. All we have is the relationship around the values of the company and what we bring to the customer every day. And we all have to own it.

Values create context rather than rules. Like the front of the jigsaw puzzle box, values give your staff the 'how' in achieving purpose at work. Values act as a compass that you commit to using consistently as a guide on your journey and to decision making at work.

Values help:

- leaders more quickly establish commonalities with one other which lead them to help each other solve their problems;
- people know where they stand in a company and make decisions with confidence;
- people make good judgement calls in any situation where values have been considered in the decision making; and
- the overall environment feel like a safe place in which to speak up and contribute, where everyone accepts each other more on an equal level regardless of the organisational hierarchy.

If you don't already have a set of core values then start to think about the following:

- What do you stand for as a business?
- What do you care about?
- How would your competitors describe you?
- How would your customers describe you?
- How would your suppliers describe you?

At the end of the day, we are creatures who crave social bonds and connections. Values connect people and unlock ways for employees and leaders to give meaning to why we do things the way we do.

It is easy for us to ask employees to be their best when serving customers, once the best has been described to them in terms of values.

SACRED GOLD

I worked with a leader recently who was having a few problems with some of his key store managers. When we got into the situation more deeply, he realised he never took the time to get to know his team and learn why they wanted to come and work where they worked. As a result, they were disengaged and dragging the results of the whole organisation down.

To address the issue, we went through the following three steps:

1. The leader wrote down all the names of the people he wanted to connect with more at work.

2. He then arranged a time for a coffee with each of them in an environment that was away from their store and asked them what were their current problems or challenges at work.
3. He then asked them where they saw themselves in six months, one year and three years from now.

What was revealed in those conversations was a much deeper sense of purpose from each of the employees on what they were searching for in the workplace than the leader ever thought.

This information is sacred gold between a leader and employee; not to be used to manipulate, but to help you understand someone far greater – what makes them tick?

So if you are unclear of your organisation's purpose, ask someone who might have the answer. What a great conversation to get started in your business!

Twelve key dimensions

Understanding how your particular job contributes to your company's mission or purpose can be a powerful measure of emotional satisfaction, as Gallup discovered in a multi-year research project.

Gallup identified 12 key dimensions – the Q^{12} – that it suggests are the core drivers of employee retention, wellbeing and overall happiness in the workplace. The Q^{12} are framed as questions to measure what Gallup considers are the most important elements of employee engagement, as follows:

1. Do you know what is expected of you at work?
2. Do you have the materials and equipment to do your work right?
3. At work, do you have the opportunity to do what you do best every day?

4. In the last seven days, have you received recognition or praise for doing good work?

5. Does your supervisor, or someone at work, seem to care about you as a person?

6. Is there someone at work who encourages your development?

7. At work, do your opinions seem to count?

8. Does the mission/purpose of your company make you feel your job is important?

9. Are your associates (fellow employees) committed to doing quality work?

10. Do you have a best friend at work?

11. In the last six months, has someone at work talked to you about your progress?

12. In the last year, have you had opportunities to learn and grow?

Whether your employees can articulate it or not, whether it's something really big and far-reaching, or something tangible and short-term, each of your employees will have a deeper intrinsic motivation for getting out of bed each day and coming to work, and it's not money. In fact, it's the 12 key dimensions listed above that contribute far more to building an engaged workforce than money ever will.

As leaders, we must never lose sight of the fact that happy employees equal happy customers.

Reflecting on purpose

1. What is the purpose of your organisation?

2. What do you love about working there?

3. How do you communicate this to your team?

4. Have you got values that you live by to help you achieve the purpose of your organisation? What are they?

5. What is the impact of your purpose having on employees, customers, humanity?

6. How does your organisation share its purpose, internally and externally?

7. If you do not have a purpose, what is it that you care about most as a business and how is that having an impact on people?

UNSUNG HERO: Bendigo Bank

*"Believe in your brand, and your
customers believe in it too"*

Australia's fifth-largest retail bank has more than 7,200 staff helping 1.6 million customers. So growing a customer-centric culture has been no mean feat!

During my time spent with Ian Jackman, Head of Customer Voice at Bendigo Bank, he revealed that the company's 160-year success is due to its vision – "To be Australia's most customer-connected bank" – and the process it uses to communicate that to customers, communities, staff, partners and stakeholders. The company vision underpins every decision made by the senior leaders in head office through to the frontline employees in a branch. The vision provides clarity for employees – describing why the company is doing what it is doing – and highlights how central each and every customer is to every touchpoint across the organisation. The organisation firmly believes that banks feed into prosperity, not off it – and this sentiment is even emblazoned across office windows: "successful customers create a successful community, which creates a successful bank, but only in that order". Bendigo Bank is sure about its purpose and so are its employees – you'll see how this leads to success after reading this Unsung Hero case study.

Haylee Doering, Preston Branch Manager, explains how the vision cascades down to the frontline and is felt in the everyday practices of her team:

> We make sure that 'what we stand for' is a constant
> conversation in our branch. We do this by talking about

the customer experiences that we have as a team. In our branch meetings, which take place twice a week, we have a section of our meeting called 'peak and pit'. A peak would be a really great story that is aligned to our purpose and customer values and a pit would be an experience that did not go so well.

We share these ideas to discuss how to overcome them and more importantly to see if there is any further support needed from the team to continually improve these customer experiences. This is how our common belief of why we are here at the branch translates every day for us.

The surest way to influence customers to trust your brand and your organisation is to create an emotional connection between your customers and your employees. When you look at the results from Qualtrics at the end of this case study, you will see how successful Bendigo Bank has been at this.

The company's employees create trust with their customers because they truly believe in what they are doing and this intention is felt by customers through their interactions. As Ian explains:

If we look at who we are, and what we represent in the community – the heart of what the business model is – it's about shared value across customers, communities, partners and the bank. It's about trust in who we are. And trust is something that we have worked hard to build through our actions over a long period of time.

During recent times, the financial services industry has been undergoing a lot of change, through innovation as well as through inquiries into the behaviours, culture and actions of financial services organisations. Trust is really important for our customers. We believe that our actions speak louder than words and that this helps to differentiate us from our competitors.

So how do you consistently maintain this level of trust in a modern world where each customer experience across multiple platforms and multiple channels of engagement is different and ever-changing? Customers who call the bank, who go into a branch, who hop online or choose to do all three, still demand consistency from a company – regardless of the time, location, employee or channel.

What I liked about Ian's explanation of consistency is that he is realistic about what can and cannot be achieved in a large-scale organisation with multiple sites and a workforce of thousands of unique human beings:

> I think we have to understand what we mean by consistency. And you start with what the customer expects, and what they're seeking from us. No matter how they choose to interact, any time, any place, anyhow, we have to be there and ready to meet their needs. But I think consistency is an interesting one. I'd call it consistent quality of experience. Because the experience itself might differ, based on the circumstance and the need, and the context. And that's okay. But there should be consistent quality and personalisation about the experience.

One of the ways to achieve this consistent quality experience is to place more effort on showing employees how to build rapport and relationships with customers, and less effort on mandating steps of service.

Bendigo Bank refers to several ways in which it continually demonstrates 'how' to personalise and nurture relationships with the customer.

Julie Dillon, Senior Manager of Customer Intelligence, manages a team tasked with sharing the truth about the service levels in the business: the unfiltered messages. They are the go-to for learning and reinforcing what best practice looks like in service. They make sure the customer voice is recognised and heard at all levels of leadership and in real time. She says:

> We don't just report what we think the senior people want to hear. We tell them what's really happening.
>
> The Customer Intelligence team is seen as extremely valuable to the whole organisation. We catch all feedback, we categorise and analyse it and we look at what emerging issues there are or any trends. With every compliment that we hear of, we go back to that frontline person and we make sure that their leader and their line of management is fully aware of that positive experience.

What struck me most about Bendigo Bank was the transparency and accessibility of information to employees about how they are performing in the eyes of the customer.

The bank captures real-time feedback from ongoing pulse surveys instead of monthly updates, and it has self-service dashboards where employees can access stories from customers to help engage the large workforce. To complement the customer perspective, the bank also conducts regular employee pulse checks. Alongside a range of cultural benefits, this enables staff to suggest opportunities to improve processes, systems and customer engagement. Julie says:

> Our management and frontline staff want to see what's going on broadly in their region or business. They truly want to see what customers are saying about us and what the themes of discontent are, for example, in a particular area of our service. We've got people in the organisation who read every single piece of content that comes in, because our people are really interested to understand what that pulse and that voice is out there. It reinforces what we are doing well and to find ways to continually improve the customer experience.

So if you want consistent quality experiences from your service teams, then you must be consistent with your communications, feedback and conversations and make information available to all employees so that they can absorb the customer's direct viewpoint.

In comparison, I see companies measuring customer service effort, satisfaction, Net Promoter Score, loyalty and customer voice with varied weightings alongside financial and risk measures. What gets measured is what gets managed and the measures of success define what is important for a workforce to focus on.

The customer service metrics of Bendigo Bank sit alongside other important metrics and they define their measures of success and outcomes as follows with equal weighting:

- Net customer numbers growth
- NPS
- Partner experience index
- eNPS
- Diversity and inclusion score

- Gender diversity in the senior leadership group
- Lending growth
- Net interest margin
- Cost to assets
- Cash earnings per share.

The prominence, importance and depth of the customer metrics are different to other banks, as Ian explains:

> If you look at any of the typical banks, their metrics are largely and primarily driven by financial and risk, hard portfolio dollar-type measures. We certainly have those because they are important. But sitting alongside that, and of equal standing, are our customer measures of success.

> Over the last 12 months we have rolled out a new customer metrics framework, which is more customer-centred and has deep levels of granularity. We have three core categories: Attract, Please and Grow. Attract is about brand awareness and the goodwill people put into our brand. Whether they would consider us, and whether we're relevant in what we have to offer. Our 'Please' metrics are sourced directly from the voice of our customers and assess the quality of experience that we are delivering. This includes advocacy, satisfaction, our responsiveness to their needs and their overall satisfaction.

Focusing on customer service measurements alongside financial performance, as part of regular team meetings, reinforces the idea that what is measured is what is important in the workplace. Haylee adds:

> Staff know to expect sales focus agenda items in weekly meetings; however, we like to shift the focus to a new conversation around the customer relationship that I think staff value more because it's something that they can

influence positively and continue to improve on. By talking about the peaks and pits of an experience it constantly reinforces to the staff which actions and behaviours create positive, quality experiences and which fall short. It's learning and improving through sharing experience, and staff love that approach.

Distinct parts of an organisation latch on to different measures which are meaningful and resonate with their role, and their ability to shift the dial on those metrics. But it is also important to join the dots to other business drivers such as financial and risk which help to give extra weight to the importance of customer service and how, ultimately, a better customer experience leads to broader success across the organisation.

Measuring customer outcomes in numerous ways means that for the organisation as a whole, customer service becomes more relevant to more people.

MINDSET MOMENTS

1. Bendigo Bank leads a service culture with purpose.
2. It lives by a vision that underpins every action it takes as an organisation.
3. It is clear on why it shares information and how it connects to other business drivers.
4. It is clear on why it measures various parts of the customer's experience.
5. The end result is that when it leads with intention, it has been successful in creating an emotional connection with its people and the customers they interact with.

6. When employees believe in their leaders, this trust directly impacts their actions, which directly (and positively) impacts the results achieved.

Customer metrics

- Customer feedback, monthly trends and insights (available on a self-service dashboard for staff to view themselves).
- Customer satisfaction (by Qualtrics).
- Customer handling happiness (how well staff responded to and resolved customer needs).

Below is a table showing the customer metric framework of all areas that Bendigo Bank measures, collates and tracks. These metrics are reviewed at monthly senior meetings and at Executive and Board level.

Attract	Please	Grow
Brand awareness The brand value results in interest and consideration of our products and services	**Advocacy** Our customers are recommending up to others	**Reach** We are reaching and engaging with our target customers and thereby increasing our overall share of the market
Brand sentiment There are strong positive perceptions about our brand and our differentiation in the eyes of potential and current customers	**Satisfaction** Our customers are happy with the overall experience and solutions that we are providing	**Acquisition** We are growing by acquiring new customers

Attract	Please	Grow
Interest The brand value results in interest and consideration of our products and services	**Ease** We are making it simple and easy for customers to connect with us and fulfil their needs	**Attrition** We are minimising the number of customers who are leaving us
Relevance Our solutions and services are relevant and aligned to the needs of potential customers	**Responsiveness** We are responding to customer needs in a manner and timeliness that meets their expectations	**Depth** We are actively deepening our relationship with existing customers

Note: the Please metrics (middle column in the table above) are all sourced directly from customers via pulse surveys that are issued weekly and also following specific interactions.

Awards

- #1 Forrester's Australian Customer Experience Index (2016, 2017, 2018).
- Highest customer satisfaction (Roy Morgan Single Source, 12 months to March 2018).
- Top 10 (and only Bank) in the Roy Morgan Net Trust Score.
- Most reputable Australian Bank in the AMR Corporate Reputation Index.
- RFi Group, Australian Business Banking Awards: Best Non-Major Business Bank.
- Mozo People's Choice Awards 2017: Rated Top Bank – Outstanding Customer Satisfaction, Excellent Customer Service, Highly Trusted, Staff Friendliness, Most Recommended, Excellent Banking App, Customer Satisfaction – Everyday Banking, Customer Satisfaction – Credit Cards.

What its customers say

- When asked about the importance of factors in a general pulse survey, Customer Service is the top-rated response, with 98% of respondents indicating this is 'quite' (17%) or 'very' (81%) important. This is followed by 'Low Fees and Charges' (95%) and 'Strong Corporate Values' (94%).
- 86% of the customers then responded that Bendigo Bank is meeting (38%) or exceeding (48%) expectations in relation to Customer Service.
- Text and sentiment analysis is run from the survey verbatim responses, which helps the bank to understand the key topics mentioned by customers and the level of positivity or negativity overall and in relation to each topic. Emerging themes and topics which drive negative sentiment help to drive focus and actions around the things that need to be improved. Customer Service is the strongest driver of positive sentiment from the text analytics, followed by Friendly and Helpful Staff.

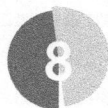

Mindset 6: Practice

Knowledge without practice is useless;
practice without knowledge is dangerous.

CONFUCIUS

It was 2017, the day after the Australian Open men's finals. One of tennis fans' most-loved superstars Roger Federer had just taken the title yet again. It was an epic four-hour match and I was working behind the scenes, so I was privy to insights not seen on TV.

I heard that even after Federer took out the title, he was out on the courts the very next day practising post-win. I thought, "Surely he can spare one day off from practising his forehand technique?"

After speaking to someone who knows Federer well, I learned that the reason he practised the next day was because he was practising a behaviour, not a technical skill. As they say, 'You are only as good as your last performance', so he didn't want to become complacent about what it takes to be a winner.

In much the same way, service leaders must continue to practise their behaviours, no matter how good the results say they are.

The business world is constantly evolving and changing, which impacts and changes the needs and wants of your customers, as well as those of your employees. Our role as leaders is to keep up with these demands that surround us and our people – and sometimes this requires us to try different things, put ourselves outside of our comfort zone, so we are constantly improving our performance and the performance of our people.

One risk in business is that good levels of performance feel comfortable and familiar, limiting our need to change, grow or do something different. The associated risk is that our business results will then not only plateau, but they may decline, while the world around us continually changes. Adequate is not excellent.

Good is no longer good enough.

PLAY A CONTINUOUS GAME

Conscious leaders create a cumulative advantage by lifting the performance of their employees, not by doing what they always did but by continually looking at ways to do and be better.

Often, we hear leaders talk about their years in service like it's a badge of honour. Yes, time spent in an industry working with the same clientele, in the same market and working with the same products makes you knowledgeable, but how good are you at leading in this field of work simply with knowledge?

What do you practise and how does this practice make you better?

In his book *Outliers*, Malcolm Gladwell wrote that "ten thousand hours is the magic number of greatness". Gladwell thus coined the term known as the 10,000-hour rule.

Anders Ericsson, a psychologist who researched and germinated the idea of the 10,000-hour rule, explained his theory when being interviewed by Daniel Goleman in Goleman's book *Focus*:

> You don't get benefits from mechanical repetition, but by adjusting your execution over and over to get closer to your goal. You have to tweak the system by pushing, allowing for more errors at first as you increase your limits.

In addition, Goleman says that the 10,000-hour rule is necessary for great performance but not sufficient. Paying attention while practising makes a crucial difference:

> When practice occurs while we are paying full attention, and not being distracted or focusing anywhere else but on the task, neuroplasticity occurs, which is the strengthening of old brain circuits and building new ones for a skill. This is why experts say that practice leads to skill.

So whether it's to get closer to a goal, make something new feel easy over time or simply to improve your performance – practice mindfully and with purpose rather than mindlessly and without purpose. Be like Federer who, the day after his Grand Slam win, practised to remind himself that he is only as good as his last performance.

Regardless of how well he practised that day, it was the effort and showing up to practice that counted.

Practise in the same way you always have and you'll get the same results you always have.

HOW HUNGRY ARE YOU?

One of the surest ways to determine if your organisation has adopted a service mindset is to assess the appetite for growth among your teams. Most people value opportunities to develop themselves, they value knowledge and learning new skills. The workplace is an obvious place to provide such people-centred growth.

Carol Dweck, the author of *Mindset*, says:

> When you learn new things, these tiny connections in the brain actually multiply and get stronger. The more you challenge your mind to learn, the more your brain cells grow. Then, things that you once found very hard or even impossible – like speaking a foreign language or doing algebra – seem to become easy. The result is a stronger, smarter brain.

And James Clear, an author and keen observer of people and routines, echoes the Roger Federer example above in his explanation of deliberate practice:

Deliberate practice is purposeful and systematic. While regular practice might include mindless repetitions, deliberate practice requires focused attention and is conducted with the specific goal of improving performance.

Practice isn't supposed to be comfortable.

Imagine if one day you were asked to do something you were not familiar with. For example, someone asked you to brush your teeth when holding your toothbrush in your other hand. Intuitively, this doesn't feel right. It feels like you will not get the same results as you do when using your preferred hand.

What if you were to learn that by brushing your teeth with the other hand you would get better results eventually? Initially you may be resistant to this alternative approach. Learning something for the first time can feel clunky and awkward, almost like you are a kid again. It would be easy for you to quit and go back to what you have always done, use the familiar hand.

However, thanks to science, we know that the brain is built to form habits and rewiring these habits is a tricky, ongoing task. Changing habits requires steady, consistent effort. It's pushing through the first few attempts that feel hard, which then takes you to feeling a sense of progress – no matter how small that progress may be – which eventually leads to some breakthroughs.

Progress is critical to feeling a sense of achievement, no matter how small or large that achievement is. When we have a sense of achievement we release a hormone called dopamine, known as one of the 'happiness hormones' and also referred to as the 'reward' hormone. Dopamine gives us a surge of pleasure when we achieve goals, desires or needs. Hence when we make progress we want to keep going, and it's through practice that we begin to grow and shine. People with low levels of dopamine may suffer from self-doubt, procrastination and lack of enthusiasm.

When you feel that first flash of progress, this is a critical point at which to not give up but keep with the technique, keep persevering and learning from the actual practice, knowing that eventually you will get to a more comfortable place. You have to stretch yourself to be better than you were – it will just take some practice.

With perseverance comes growth,
both in skill and confidence.

Leverage your best assets

A client of mine spoke to me candidly one day about how ineffective he felt his senior leadership team were. He referred to the business as reactive, that they didn't have enough time to deal with the important stuff and that they didn't have the right resources (I'm sure you can relate to at least some of this).

While some of these statements may have been true, what became clear over a period of time was that, in actual fact, his leaders were not practising in the areas from which they would gain most leverage.

In the service sector, where you rely on humans to serve your customers, you will get the most impact from your teams if you spend most of your time with your people.

The client realised that his finance leader spent all day in an office crunching numbers, looking at spreadsheets and sending emails, instead of looking after his team of 15 people. His product leader spent all day looking at spreadsheets, reading supplier contracts and emails and making product decisions, instead of looking after his team of six people.

Both leaders spent less than 20% of their time with the people who had the power to make or break the business.

Remember, your job is to be responsible for the people responsible for the results. Service leaders who think that they are wholly responsible for the results, usually have forgotten they have a team there to help them achieve the results.

As service leaders, you must never stop practising your people skills.

THE BEST WAY TO PRACTISE IS EVERY DAY

The best way to practise is every day. Putting in a volume of work is relevant to the individual who is practising, as well as at an organisational level where you are trying to shift the dial on a new procedure or a new standard in service. It's the sum of many parts all coming together and practising intentionally and relentlessly that eventually shifts that dial.

As you will see for Healthscope, the Unsung Hero discussed at the end of this chapter, it was the deliberate refining of daily habits and committing to large volumes of work that eventually led to a new benchmark of best practice. The decision to keep improving is what has led Healthscope to exceed national standards of patient care in a hospital.

A great quantity of work will feel overwhelming if it is not broken down into bite-size pieces. The bite-size pieces then feed into a larger goal that everyone in the organisation is consciously working towards.

The idea around doing and repeating a volume of work also serves as a reminder of the usefulness of hearing things, seeing things, doing things and experiencing things more than once.

Take reading a book, for example. I can read a book in January, highlighting in yellow the bits of the book that resonate with me and seem profound at the time. Twelve months later I can pick up that same book with a green highlighter and I notice that I am highlighting different sections of the book that now resonate with me and seem profound.

The book hasn't changed; I have. It's the same content, but at the time I perceived it in a different way.

So if you really want to commit to developing a customer service culture, remember that in your ongoing gatherings, training sessions, lunch-and-learn forums – whatever mode of learning and development works for your business – you can never focus on your topics of interest too much.

You can never get tired of focusing on the same issues or topics if they are spread out over time and delivered in different ways. People will always have a different experience and may find they walk away from the same content they learned a few months earlier with a new learning. Practice will keep you, your employees and your organisation heading towards a cumulative advantage, ahead of the curve, sustaining great results with customers.

Don't be afraid to repeat your development programs; repeating them will serve to deepen your practice of being a great service leader and will inspire and influence your employees' practice of meaningful customer service.

There are many ways to practise service; think about what best suits you and your staff, without simply keeping everyone in their comfort zones. What's important is to make practice a habitual element in your organisation. Here are a few examples:

- **Practise from the start.** Start with onboarding: get people on the tools and in front of customers, regardless of their role, in their first week or two.
- **Practise when your customers and competitors are sleeping:** Make time for after-hours training sessions.
- **Practise in small chunks throughout a day:** Try tools such as 'skill pills' that are quick injections or skill refreshers which can be done in a 10-15 minute team briefing or huddle, or can be included at the end of a weekly meeting.
- **Practise in large gatherings:** At team conferences, roadshows and events. This will reinforce the service expectations of your culture in a different environment, and in a more engaging way. Large gatherings are great places for people to learn from others and hear the same expectations differently.
- **Practise in pairs:** Why don't more organisations adopt the buddy system? When you have identified the true champions of customer service and the employees who need a little help, pair them up and empower the champions to lift their buddies' performance by letting them experience first-hand what it takes to deliver exceptional service.

FAILURE IS PART OF PRACTICE

In the service industry we are sometimes afraid of messing up, especially if we are 'performing' in view of the customer. A common scenario we've all seen is when an employee has a customer problem they cannot solve and so they call for a manager to help them. Now the manager has been introduced as the hero of the scene, hoping to provide all the solutions and show the employee how it's done. This is a tricky situation to find yourself in if you are a leader who believes you should have all the answers and in this situation you do not.

Fortunately, customers are more forgiving than we realise. They don't expect leaders to have all the answers; however, they do expect leaders to be honest and find the answers for them. If we see someone trying to learn, be better and improve, we are likely to admire that trait. Think about when you are a customer and you witness a company putting in continuous effort and willingness to be better than yesterday.

Customers value transparency and they appreciate it when they see brands behaving as the leaders in their sector. These days we are far more forgiving as customers if we know an individual did their best. We are far more admiring of a brand when we see individuals practising to be their best.

Talk about your failures.
Learn how to be better from them.

The most successful customer service programs are those that have a place for ongoing dialogue between leaders who are all practising new behaviours.

Some companies choose to have an agenda item in their weekly meetings where they ask a specific question about something that the leaders are focusing on, and what have been their experiences of or learnings from that. Webinars are also another great forum through which to share what has not worked and hear from peers and colleagues what their learnings have been and what modifications they have tried.

The result of sharing with others is that the culture becomes more resilient to failures and encourages people to keep practising.

Whenever I feel I have failed in something I always ask myself:

- Who says it's a failure?
- Why did it fail?
- What was not gained?

This then usually leads me to realise that this 'failure' was simply a way of learning what to do next.

This is why I like to replace the word 'fail' with 'experiment'. When you try something new for the first time and the result was not what you set out to achieve, so what? Tweak it, learn from it, dust yourself off and try again.

Remember to experiment, a lot.

TAKE A STEP, TODAY

The origin of the word practice comes from the medieval Latin *practizare*, meaning 'to perform, carry out'. You want people in your workplace who are willing to 'perform' and show up before they are completely ready, who are willing to grow and give 100%.

Throughout this book, we have looked at certain behaviours that will lift the performance of service leaders, like you, with the corresponding impact on your frontline that they consistently deliver great service. If you were to choose any one of these behaviours to develop more deeply, it would require motivation and an amount of effort to get you going.

The hardest step is starting the task, then the issue is maintaining a commitment to keep going.

When you look at starting to practice, it is helpful to understand why you want to develop a new behaviour or skill in the first place.

For example, imagine I was told that I was too direct with my staff and that their engagement levels were noticeably dropping and their performance was impacting the service results. Potentially I could improve this by leading more with questions. Knowing that coaching is not my natural leadership style, it would require me to really commit to practising leading with more questions.

First, what I would need to get clear on is: Why would it be helpful if I lead with more questions? By telling my staff what to do not only limits their growth and development, but it also makes my job harder because the team become dependent on me to make all the decisions, even when I am not there. Once you can see the benefit, not only to others but to yourself, you are ready to sign up for the challenge!

Set yourself daily or weekly targets around the service improvements you wish to make in the business. Start by looking at behaviours and the impact that improving those behaviours would have on your team and your customers.

Action precedes clarity. The sooner you start practising your desired mindsets you will learn more, see more and achieve more clarity around how to be more effective in what it is you are practising.

You learn best by experiencing it yourself.

Reflecting on practice

1. What behaviours could you practise more to help you grow? What about your team?

2. Other than growth, what else would be the benefits to the business, your team and customers if you all developed these behaviours?

3. What would be a realistic volume of work for your team to put in, when developing a behaviour? What specific goal could be set to see some positive impact?

4. How do you share failures in your organisation?

5. How much time is dedicated to practising people skills versus technical skills in your organisation?

UNSUNG HERO: Healthscope

"Make time to practise"

Any business today is impacted by the economy, market, competition, location and the changing needs of society in general. Believe it or not, hospitals are no different.

Our ageing population is driving the demand for more hospital beds in Australia, while there is a shortage of nurses as well as a nursing workforce that is also ageing. The whole sector is under pressure yet, like any other business, hospitals are trying to make a profit.

One of the key drivers in business is the happiness and engagement of employees and how that translates into the treatment of customers – in a hospital, that means patients.

Interviewing Cathy Jones, National Manager of Quality and Compliance at Healthscope, I was inspired to learn that hospitals are making fundamental efforts to improve patient care beyond the national standard. They view these endeavours as, not only aiding faster recovery of patients while in hospital, but also achieving a healthier bottom line, as complications such as infections are very costly.

For example, patients are invited to rate the 'overall quality of treatment and care' on a five-point scale, as part of the post-discharge feedback survey. Since Healthscope began to focus on reporting its scores more frequently (monthly), with a dashboard benchmarking between hospitals and wards, it has seen a marked improvement in this core measure over time. The dashboard shows scores in real time.

Healthscope hospitals go beyond the clinical needs of every patient to make sure that best practice always continues. So Healthscope is my final Unsung Hero due to how it has excelled in creating a practice mindset in its employees.

As Cathy explains:

> We have clinical leadership in hospitals, which makes sure the relevant procedures and policies are followed, that staff are doing the right practices every day. However, we also practise how our staff care for patients. We do training and education with the lead nurses to show them how to use a proper person-centred care model. This too requires practice.

With over 40 hospitals around Australia and more than 18,000 employees, Healthscope's staff development and training has three objectives:

1. Redefine what best practice is in Healthscope hospitals.
2. Never rest on your laurels and continually practise to improve.
3. Be realistic about how best to deliver messages and training in a hospital environment where staff resources are stretched.

Patient outcome, patient experience, staff experience and financial performance are the four factors that define best practice at a Healthscope hospital. The best-performing individual hospitals in the network have a balanced weighting of all four.

One of Healthscope's innovative approaches to best practice is its Mystery Patient program:

> The mystery patient program is based on standard mystery shopper principles. We pick a real patient who is scheduled to come in to hospital; either a staff member who was scheduled

to go in to hospital for a procedure or a patient who we knew well that we felt we could approach and ask to participate. We call it a patient journey. This includes the patient diarising their journey in more detail than usual. We are aiming to find out the best parts of the care and the worst parts of the care, as well as the duplication, the waste, the rework.

This program has helped us to include material in our training programs to help nursing staff understand what it must be like from a patient's perspective.

We have had the same patient in three different hospitals (this can take time) and so then our benchmarking and learnings are not jaded by different hospital practices but rather looking at an overall consistency of emotional connection and experience of feeling cared for.

As a senior leader, Cathy has participated in this program herself as has Healthscope's managing director/CEO. She emphasises the importance of leaders going to the sites and getting a sense of what is actually happening in the hospitals. It's too easy to view a business from a high-rise building in a city as just numbers and forget that we are actually dealing with humans.

Cathy comments:

I make sure I get out to the hospitals often. I talk to the frontline staff every couple of months and go out to different hospitals doing training on the ward. I do this so I am in touch with the coal face of the business. In particular, if we are trying to introduce some new customer service strategies, I can see that maybe we need to remove some other tasks first, so get rid of some unnecessary rework in order to free up a bit more time.

What is refreshing when listening to Cathy is that the practice in leadership never stops, no matter how high up the food chain you are. Keeping close to the customers (their patients) is a key activity for Cathy in order to continually get close to the actual experiences and potential gaps in the performance of the staff.

Being seen as a leader on the floor is certainly a behaviour of proactive leadership, says Cathy:

> We require our nurses to do time-based rounding of the patients. So instead of just responding when the patient presses a call bell, they pop in every hour or in some cases every two hours to check if the patient needs any help or care. This proactive approach actually saves the nurses time and also tells the patients that we care about them.

Compare this to a very different environment like a McDonald's restaurant. When the same activity is employed by shift leaders, it is called the 'travel path'. The point of this is to get an overview of what is needed out on the floor in every area of the restaurant and deal with it accordingly before it becomes a complaint, hazard or issue for customers.

Cathy says Healthscope is very focused on making sure its senior staff in the hospitals lead by example and continue to practise tasks and procedures that their teams practise:

> For the ward nurse manager, there are a lot of tasks occupying their time. But even if it's not the highest priority, it's really important for them to also be seen in the patient rooms, rounding on their patients daily. This gives the patient the chance to meet the manager and provide feedback on their treatment and care, as well as showing leadership for the nurses on the floor.

Great strategies such as proactive time-based rounding of patients ensure mediocrity does not creep into a team's performance.

Clinical leadership is an area that hospitals practise with their eyes closed. Nurses are used to standards and procedures changing and having to adapt, as technology and medicine evolve their practices. Cathy explained that Healthscope also focuses equally on practising skills to match the mindset of a patient:

> The experience of a patient is so tied up with what happens to their own body and health. But as well as worrying about how they're going to recover, they have the added worries about their families and who's feeding their dog at home, and so on. These are different factors that you sometimes do not get in other industries – here you are serving customers who are basically at their most vulnerable. The absolute best of the nurses, those who are showing the sharpest empathy, are the ones who realise how this feels – that the patient in the bed is wanting to feel as though they are their most important patient; a favourite.

When I visit my local café, I hope that the way I am served is unique for me. I know when I have witnessed the same level of attentiveness and care from my regular barista towards another customer, I start to doubt that I am their most important customer. It's a fabulous way of thinking about a service mindset.

How do your staff perform so they make the customer feel like they are a favourite, and what do they need to practise to reinforce this?

One of the biggest shifts in best practice for Healthscope were the changes they made with bedside handovers. This improvement required commitment and practice like never before. Previously nurses would hand over their shift to the next nurse in an impersonal room away from the patients, which meant they couldn't respond to any patient requests or queries if they arose.

Cathy explains:

> One of the methods of moving towards a patient-centred care model is to move away from nursing station handover to bedside handover. Each nurse is in charge of maybe five patients and in the ideal world Josie hands over to Fran, with the two of them at the bedside of the patient. You involve the patient. You find out all sorts of things at the bedside, can check all the tubes, the equipment and you can check the chart and make sure the medication is right. It is also a great methodology to reinforce to the patient some important points. When a patient hears nurses talking together, patients tell us that they nearly always find out something they didn't know before.

This methodology threw up many obstacles for Healthscope initially, and it was met with resistance to the change. The intention for changing the handover was to improve the customer service for their patients, decrease errors and involve patients in decision making about their treatment and care. To support the change, videos were created to highlight how time-efficient bedside handover is and to inspire staff to not see this as an obstacle but rather an improvement.

Nurses initially saw this new focus as extra work. "I can't do this as well as my other work," was the reaction. Cathy continued:

We had to show the nurses that it was simply a different approach, not an additional task. We had to explain to the nurses how eventually this methodology would save them time because the patient will be much happier, you will get fewer complaints and more engaged patients who will not leave it to the last minute to tell you that they need help to get to the toilet, for example.

It has also forced nurses to be more aware of what they say and how they say it, in view of their patients. The tireless commitment and practice from the nurses to change their handover methodology meant that they eventually got to a place where what once seemed hard and messy was now easy and practical. They felt re-energised.

We really have worked hard on getting our nurses to communicate better with the patients. This change of handover procedure meant that nurses not only needed to practise a new way of doing the handover, ie location and sequence of communication, they also needed to practise delivering their messages with care and empathy.

Empathy in a hospital is paramount. Healthscope has approached this mindset by identifying champions, acting out role plays and scenarios in training and providing videos as well as scripts to assist nurses in various patient scenarios.

No matter what your industry or environment, it's important to continually practise and encourage empathy.

MINDSET MOMENTS

1. Healthscope has created a service culture in which its staff make time to practise.

2. It is committed to its training efforts and materials, leaving few excuses for leaders to not try.
3. It doesn't stop at service levels of minimum competency and quality, but rather strives to exceed national standards.
4. Healthscope understands the mindset of its patients (customers) and has adopted transparent practices that involve patients.
5. It continually refreshes and re-energises its staff by insisting training and development is part of their core tasks and by showing how little effort and time it takes, in the overall scheme of things.

Customer metrics

- NPS (for patients/customers) (by Qualtrics).
- Staff survey – Sustainable Employee Engagement score.
- Key Performance Indicators for complaints; meaning the time it takes to acknowledge and the time to the final response.
- Attendance rates at customer service education and training.

Final thoughts

As you've seen over the course of this book, service is simple when we get it right.

The trouble is that we make it overly complex. We create systems and processes that, while designed to help us, often hinder us instead. They stop us delivering the service that our customers deserve. They stop us from making real and long-lasting connections in the world.

So take a minute to ponder:

Where are your systems and processes getting
in the way of humans serving humans?

Service is an honour, a privilege. We need to bring our service back to a place of love and connection. We need to have a simple and focused approach.

A common theme in the Unsung Heroes' stories is that you must give equal focus to the employee experience and the customer experience. I predict, based on what I am seeing with industry leaders across multiple sectors and what I learn from companies such as Qualtrics, that the employee Net Promoter Score (eNPS) will be just as important an indicator of service performance in years to come as the original NPS that measures customer satisfaction.

Many organisations in Australia, like some we have read about in this book, are starting to not only track but interpret the correlation of happiness to customer service for employees (the eNPS) as well as customers (the NPS).

How well do you treat your employees?
How much is your treatment of them dictating
their treatment of your customers?

Change starts with you.

It's a service mindset that you need to lead with, not a sequence of service. It's the kind of service mindset that is with you no matter who you are with or where you are; it's a way of being and not something you do when you put your uniform on.

Throughout this book we have unpacked six mindsets that lead to ways of being, rather than things to do. Learning a mindset begins by first having greater self-awareness, which will give you clarity on how your thoughts impact your actions.

When you have greater awareness of how you are leading with **empathy, questions, energy, heart, purpose** and **practice**, you are then consciously able to choose better actions that will yield better results.

Which mindset, from the six explored in this book,
have you decided needs your attention most?

When it comes to service – connecting to your customers, gaining loyalty, building trust and growing a brand and a business – leaders steer the ship.

When a leader looks at ways to be of service to their employees and their customers, they have the ability to transform their approach to their work, their relationships and help humanity in a multitude of ways.

We cannot expect our teams to follow us and our customers to like us, and come back and see us again, if we are not willing to practise a service mindset ourselves.

When you change, the world around you changes.

The only question left to ask yourself is:

How will you change?

Work with me

Do you believe that service is a mindset? Are you wondering how you can shift the dial in your service culture in a more upwards, positive direction? But you're not sure where to start?

Then contact us to find out about our discovery sessions where we explore:

- Where you want to take the level of service in your business
- What the current health of your service culture is like
- How to address the service mindset among your frontline leaders.

If you want to create greater self-awareness in your leaders, develop conscious leaders in a service environment, then we are destined to chat.

Contact us by email: hello@jaquiescammell.com or visit our website: www.jaquiescammell.com.

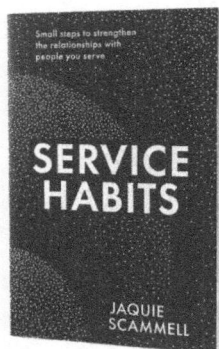

If you have enjoyed reading this book, you might like to read Jaquie's next book, *Service Habits*.

Jaquie
scammell

Small steps to strengthen
the relationships with
people you serve

SERVICE
HABITS

JAQUIE
SCAMMELL

Resources

Note: Most of the resources below are mentioned in this book. There are a few extra articles and books as a 'bonus' that aren't directly referenced but I wanted to include them as they have been useful for me and so they may be for you too.

PART I: HOW TO SERVE

CPM Australia and the ACRS Omnibus Tracker (2017) *The State of Customer Service in Australia Report. CPM Australia.* www.cpm-aus.com.au/australians-tolerance-for-poor-customer-service-is-lower-than-ever/

1. Service is human

American Express and Ebiquity (2014) *Global Customer Service Barometer: Comparison of findings across markets.* http://about.americanexpress.com/news/docs/2014x/2014-Global-Customer-Service-Barometer-All.pdf

Australian Retailers Association (2018) *ARA calls for corporate tax cuts.* www.retail.org.au/news/ara-calls-corporate-tax-cuts-2/

Blodget, H. (2012) Check Out How Apple Brainwashes Its Store Employees – Turning Them Into Clapping, Smiling Zealots. *Business Insider Australia.* www.businessinsider.com.au/how-apple-trains-store-employees-2012-6

Fernandes, T. and Pedroso, R. (2016) The effect of self-checkout quality on customer satisfaction and repatronage in a retail context. *Service Business.* 11(1), 69-92.

Ford, M. (2016) *Rise of the Robots: Technology and the Threat of a Jobless Future.* Basic Books.

Goleman, D. (2006) *Social Intelligence: The New Science of Human Relationships.* Arrow.

Leberecht, T. (2015) *The Business Romantic: Give Everything, Quantify Nothing, and Create Something Greater Than Yourself.* Harper Business.

Lifeline Australia (2016) 8 out of 10 Australians say loneliness is increasing: new survey. www.lifeline.org.au/about-lifeline/media-centre/media-releases/2016-articles/8-out-of-10-australians-say-loneliness-is-increasing

Reichheld, F. (2001) *Prescription for Cutting Costs.* Bain & Company. www.bain.com/Images/BB_Prescription_cutting_costs.pdf

Reichheld, F. and Detrick, C. (2003) *Loyalty: A Prescription for Cutting Costs.* Bain & Company. www.bain.com/Images/MM_Loyalty_prescription_cutting_costs.pdf

SBS (2018) *Minimum wage: How does Australia compare to other countries?* www.sbs.com.au/yourlanguage/arabic/en/article/2018/02/22/minimum-wage-how-does-australia-compare-other-countries

World Economic Forum (2016) *The Future of Jobs: Employment, Skills and Workforce Strategy for the Fourth Industrial Revolution.* Global Challenge Insight Report. https://www.weforum.org/reports/the-future-of-jobs

2. Conscious leaders drive a service culture

Colebatch, T. (2013) Strong dollar and rising cost of labour blunt Australian edge. *The Sydney Morning Herald.* www.smh.com.au/business/strong-dollar-and-rising-cost-of-labour-blunt-australian-edge-20130623-2oqpx.html

Gallup. CliftonStrengths assessment. www.gallupstrengthscentre.com

Seligman, M. and Peterson, C. *Your Personal Character Strengths Profile.* Survey available from www.viacharacter.org

Spector, R. and McCarthy, P.D. (2012) *The Nordstrom Way to Customer Service Excellence: The Handbook For Becoming the "Nordstrom" of Your Industry.* John Wiley & Sons.

PART II: THE SIX SERVICE MINDSETS

Burrell, L. (2018) Co-Creating the Employee Experience. *Harvard Business Review.* https://hbr.org/2018/03/the-new-rules-of-talent-management#co-creating-the-employee-experience

3. Mindset 1: Empathy

Gegeckaitė, L. (2011). Factors of customer satisfaction on services. *Global Academic Society Journal: Social Science Insight*. 4 (12), 4-13.

Goleman, D. (2013) *Empathy 101*. www.danielgoleman.info/empathy-101/

Goleman, D. (2013) The Focused Leader. *Harvard Business Review*. https://hbr.org/2013/12/the-focused-leader

Pink, D. (2005) *A Whole New Mind: Why Right-brainers Will Rule the Future*. Penguin.

Schoenewolf, G. (1990) Emotional contagion: Behavioral induction in individuals and groups. *Modern Psychoanalysis*. 15, 49-61.

Trimboli, O. Clarity creates change (Deep listening thought leader). www.oscartrimboli.com

Zorfas, A. and Leemon, D. (2016) An Emotional Connection Matters More than Customer Satisfaction. *Harvard Business Review*. https://hbr.org/2016/08/an-emotional-connection-matters-more-than-customer-satisfaction

4. Mindset 2: Questions

Bregman, P. (2015) *Four Seconds: All the Time You Need to Replace Counter-Productive Habits with Ones That Really Work*. HarperCollins.

5. Mindset 3: Energy

Colan, L. J. (2008) *Engaging the hearts and minds of all your employees: How to Ignite Passionate Performance for Better Business Results*. McGraw-Hill Education.

Klaus, P. G. (1985); Chase, R. B. and Stewart, D. M. (1994) in: Reeves, C. A. and Bednar, D. A. (1995) Quality as symphony, The Cornell Hotel and Restaurant Administration Quarterly. 36 (3), 72-79. www.sciencedirect.com/science/article/pii/001088049596939E

Stewart, D. M. (2003) Piecing Together Service Quality: A Framework for Robust Service. *Production and Operations Management*. 12 (2), 246-265.

6. Mindset 4: Heart

Carnegie, D. (1936) *How to Win Friends and Influence People*. Simon & Schuster.

Godin, S. (2008) *Tribes: We need you to lead us*. Piatkus

Schoenewolf, G. (1990) Emotional contagion: Behavioral induction in individuals and groups. *Modern Psychoanalysis*. 15, 49-61.

Tatley, N. *Independent coffee shops ruling the roast in Australia*. BusinessesForSale.com. https://australia.businessesforsale.com/australian/search/food-businesses-for-sale/articles/independent-coffee-shops-ruling-the-roast-in-australia

7. Mindset 5: Purpose

Deloitte (2014) *Culture of purpose – Building business confidence; driving growth*. 2014 core beliefs & culture survey. www2.deloitte.com/us/en/pages/about-deloitte/articles/culture-of-purpose.html

Gallup (1999) Item 8: My Company's Mission or Purpose. The twelve key dimensions that describe great workgroups (part 9). *Gallup Business Journal*. http://news.gallup.com/businessjournal/505/item-companys-mission-purpose.aspx

Gallup Employee Engagement Center. Gallup Q12. https://q12.gallup.com/

Hale, B. (2011) *The Evolution of Bruno Littlemore*. Atlantic Books.

Novak, D. (2011) *Taking People with You: The Only Way to Make Big Things Happen*. Portfolio.

Sinek, S. *Start With Why*. https://startwithwhy.com/

Virgin. *Our Purpose*. www.virgin.com/virgingroup/content/our-purpose-0

8. Mindset 6: Practice

Clear, J. *Deliberate Practice: What It Is and How to Use It*. https://jamesclear.com/deliberate-practice-theory

Dweck, C. (2006) *Mindset: The New Psychology of Success*. Hachette UK.

Gladwell, M. (2008) *Outliers: The Story of Success*. Penguin.

Goleman, D. (2013) *Focus: The Hidden Driver of Excellence*. A&C Black.